The Watershed Year

The Watershed Year

Which Way Will India Go?

P. CHIDAMBARAM

BLOOMSBURY

NEW DELHI • LONDON • OXFORD • NEW YORK • SYDNEY

BLOOMSBURY INDIA
Bloomsbury Publishing India Pvt. Ltd
Second Floor, LSC Building No. 4, DDA Complex, Pocket C – 6 & 7,
Vasant Kunj, New Delhi, 110070

BLOOMSBURY, BLOOMSBURY INDIA and the Diana logo
are trademarks of Bloomsbury Publishing Plc

First published in 2024
This edition published 2024

These columns were first published in the *Indian Express*

ISBN: PB: 978-93-56407-73-2; eBook: 978-93-56408-04-3
2 4 6 8 10 9 7 5 3 1

Typeset in Baskerville MT Std by Manipal Technologies Limited
Printed and bound in India by Thomson Press India Ltd

FSC www.fsc.org MIX Paper | Supporting responsible forestry FSC® C010615

Contents

List of Abbreviations

AAP	Aam Aadmi Party
AIADMK	All India Anna Dravida Munnetra Kazhagam
ASER	Annual Status of Education Report
BE	Budget Estimate
BJD	Biju Janata Dal
BJP	Bharatiya Janata Party
BPL	below poverty line
BRS	Bharat Rashtra Samithi
CAA	Citizenship (Amendment) Act
CAD	current account deficit
CAG	Comptroller and Auditor General of India
CAPF	Central Armed Police Forces
CBI	Central Bureau of Investigation
CBSE	Central Board of Secondary Education
CCI	Competition Commission of India
CEA	Chief Economic Adviser
CM	chief minister
CMIE	Centre for Monitoring Indian Economy
CPI	consumer price index
CPI-M	Communist Party of India (Marxist)
CUET	Common University Entrance Test
CWC	Congress Working Committee
DGCI&S	Directorate General of Commercial Intelligence and Statistics
DGP	Director General of Police
DMK	Dravida Munnetra Kazhagam
DRI	Directorate of Revenue Intelligence
ECI	Election Commission of India
ED	Enforcement Directorate
EMEs	emerging market economies
EMIs	equated monthly instalments

ES	Economic Survey
EWS	economically weaker section
FAE	first advance estimates
FD	fiscal deficit
FIFA	Fédération Internationale de Football Association
FIR	first information report
FM	finance minister
GDP	gross domestic product
GNCTD	Government of National Capital Territory of Delhi
GSDP	gross state domestic product
G-sec	government securities
GST	goods and services tax
GTR	gross tax revenue
GVA	gross value addition
HoS	Head of the State
IAS	Indian Administrative Service
IB	International Baccalaureate Organization
ICSE	Indian Certificate of Secondary Education
IIMs	Indian Institutes of Management
IITs	Indian Institutes of Technology
IMF	International Monetary Fund
IPC	Indian Penal Code
IPL	Indian Premier League
IPS	Indian Police Service
IR	Indian Railways
IT	information technology
JPC	Joint Parliamentary Committee
JD(U)	Janata Dal (United)
JMM	Jharkhand Mukti Morcha
L&T	Larsen & Toubro
LAC	Line of Actual Control
LG	Lieutenant Governor
LIC	Life Insurance Corporation of India
LPG	liquefied petroleum gas
LPR	labour participation rate

MGNREGS	Mahatma Gandhi National Rural Employment Guarantee Scheme
MLA	member of the legislative assembly
MoCI	Ministry of Commerce and Industry
MoF	Ministry of Finance
MP	member of Parliament
MRP	maximum retail price
MSME	micro, small and medium enterprises
NCB	Narcotics Control Bureau
NCP	Nationalist Congress Party
NCRB	National Crime Records Bureau
NEET	National Eligibility cum Entrance Test
NEP	New Education Policy
NFHS-5	Fifth National Family Health Survey
NFSA	National Food Security Act
NGO	non-governmental organisation
NIA	National Investigation Agency
NJAC	National Judicial Appointments Commission
NMFT	No Money for Terror
NPR	National Population Register
NRC	National Register of Citizens
NSO	National Statistical Office
NTR	new tax regime
OB van	outside broadcasting van
OBC	Other Backward Classes
ODF	open defecation free
OECD	Organisation for Economic Co-operation and Development
OTR	old tax regime
OUP	Opposition Unity Platform
PLA	People's Liberation Army
PM	prime minister
PMI	purchasing managers' index
PMO	Prime Minister's Office
PRICE	People Research on India's Consumer Economy

PSUs	public sector undertakings
RE	Revised Estimate
RJD	Rashtriya Janata Dal
RSS	Rashtriya Swayamsevak Sangh
SBI	State Bank of India
SC	Scheduled Caste
SEBI	Securities and Exchange Board of India
SFIO	Serious Fraud Investigation Office
SP	Superintendent of Police
SPAD	signal passing at danger
ST	Scheduled Tribe
TCAS	train collision avoidance system
TCS	Tata Consultancy Services
TMC	Trinamool Congress
TRCs	track recording cars
UCC	Uniform Civil Code
UNCTAD	United Nations Conference on Trade and Development
UNDP	United Nations Development Programme
UPA	United Progressive Alliance
WPI	wholesale price index
WTO	World Trade Organization

Introduction

India celebrated 75 years of independence on August 15, 2022. As far as my weekly column in the *Indian Express* was concerned, it was business as usual. The column is published on Sunday every week in English and translated and published in ten Indian-language newspapers. The Bharatiya Janata Party (BJP) government at the Centre imparted a special significance to the 76th Independence Day by calling the day the beginning of Amrit Kaal (the Golden Era). Naturally, my essays turned their focus on the actions of the government during Amrit Kaal.

Many observers thought that extraordinary initiatives would be taken after August 2022 to accelerate the growth rate that had stagnated since demonetisation (2016) and worsened since COVID-19 (2020–21). I was sceptical because my enquiries did not reveal that the council of ministers was considering any new breakthrough ideas. Nor did I think that the government had any person who could think out-of-the-box and influence the prime minister with new ideas. This is the weakness of a one-person government: all other members of the government suspend their grey cells and are content to implement the decisions that they are 'given' and in the manner they are 'told'. Advisers are happy to give 'advice' that will be accepted.

I was also aware of the behaviour of a government that is in the fourth year of a five-year term. The fifth and last year is an 'election year' and the activity in that year is more political than policy-oriented or reformative. Therefore, it is the fourth year of a government that is decisive. It was so in 2012–13, the fourth year of the second term of the United Progressive Alliance (UPA-II). It was a full three years after the international financial crisis (September 2008) that had witnessed an unprecedented quantitative easing (that is, increasing the liquidity) that had turned the financial world upside down. In that year, the Manmohan Singh government battled to control inflation, contain the fiscal and current account deficits, and recoup some of the value of the rupee. Besides, in that year, major allegations of corruption were levelled against the UPA-II government, which was forced to spend its energies on countering the charges. Though the UPA-II government was able to retrieve the economic situation substantially in 2013–14, the damage had been done. The UPA lost badly in the Lok Sabha elections of 2014.

The twelve months beginning August 15, 2022 straddled the fourth and fifth years of the second term of the National Democratic Alliance (NDA-II) government. In my view, it was the make or break twelve months and I felt that the kind of governance during that period would determine the future of the government and the country. The remaining nine months would not matter so much as the previous twelve months because the nation would be in the grip of election fever. Adding to the fever would be the assembly elections in five states in November 2023. I think I was not wrong. It is the actions and inactions of the government between August 2022 and August 2023 that have, more or less, determined the image of the Narendra Modi government. These impressions will prevail until the Lok Sabha elections in April–May 2024.

So while the prime minister and the government spokespersons described the year after August 2022 as the beginning of Amrit Kaal, I viewed the year as the watershed year of the Narendra Modi government. I wrote every week examining critically the policies and actions of the government.

*

Two issues are fundamental in determining the course of a nation. One is the political system. Democracy has become a sort of portmanteau: it can hold anything ranging from the British Westminster model to China's people's democracy. Even 'lifetime' presidents claim that they were elected with an overwhelming majority in each election. Prime Minister Sheikh Hasina of Bangladesh has said, 'Democracy has a different definition that varies country to country.' It is not enough to boast that India won independence in 1947 and holds periodic elections whose outcome is decided by one-person-one-vote. That was true in 1947 and for many years thereafter. However, over the years, Indian democracy has been hollowed out and what we have now is an enfeebled and emaciated democracy. All parties have contributed to the hollowing of democracy, some driven by the desire for power, others driven by the determination to radically alter the character of the State and its relationship with the people.

I have reflected on the role played by money in elections. There was a time when Rs 50,000 was enough to fund an election campaign in an assembly constituency. A few hundred posters and a few thousand handbills would be printed; the candidate would go around the constituency in a car or van meeting people in towns and villages; and the party workers would go from house to house seeking votes. If a big leader was visiting the constituency, a public meeting would be arranged in a town that would attract a few hundred to a few thousand people, who travelled to the meeting on foot, bicycle, bullock cart or bus. The basic tools of an election campaign improved over time, but the nature of the campaign remained essentially the same though on a larger scale. My election campaigns between 1984 and 1999 followed the same pattern, only a little more elaborate every time. Even in 2004 and 2009, I stuck to the same pattern but learned some bitter lessons.

However, throughout the country, the system had changed for the worse. Increasingly, money was the major factor in an election. Money for everything from getting party workers to canvass for votes to money distributed to voters to vote for the candidate. Massive crowds were attracted to a 'rally' by providing buses, cars, food and, most importantly, money to entice them. The rally itself was technology-dominated with sound systems, lights, television screens, video cameras, music, promotional films and other technological innovations. Each rally of a big leader cost upward of a crore of rupees. As the campaign neared polling day, money was distributed to each voter. It was styled as 'booth management'. Voters did not discriminate between parties and took money from every candidate who offered money. It is debatable if the ultimate results were democratic but the process and the path were anything but democratic. The consequence of money-driven elections is that an average loyal party member cannot aspire to contest elections. Almost all candidates are wealthy or sponsored by wealthy party leaders.

After 2004, there was – and is – another driving factor: Hindutva. It is a perversion of Hinduism. Hindutva, contrary to the Hindu philosophy, treats the non-Hindu as an alien and, among the non-Hindus, treats the Muslim as an enemy. The BJP wears Hindutva on its lapel. It refused to field a Muslim candidate in the state elections held in Gujarat, Uttar Pradesh, Karnataka and some other states. Hindutva is part of the larger agenda of the BJP to establish a Hindu Rashtra in India. A BJP MP from Madhya Pradesh said, 'The basic structure of this country is Akhand Bharat Hindu Rashtra before 1192.' This agenda, I believe, includes rewriting the Constitution and emphasising the so-called oneness of the Indian people.

In several columns written from August 2022 to August 2023, I called out the overt and covert moves of the BJP to alter the political framework according to an imagined constitution that will be in tune with their concept of a Hindu Rashtra. In this behalf, the BJP has implemented some of its immediate objectives: winning the legal dispute over the place where the Babri Masjid once stood and effectively abrogating Article 370 of the Constitution. The BJP has also put the stamp of a Hindu Rashtra on the names of several cities and roads and made claims on behalf of the Hindu faith to several places of worship and structures. It is quietly pushing the idea of a Uniform Civil Code through draft legislation in BJP-ruled states. The Central government is slowly acquiring control over the education system including universities, institutions of higher learning, appointment of faculty, the curriculum and the examination system. Powers of states are being insidiously eroded. For example, appointments of vice chancellors of state universities and the director general of police (DGP) of a state require the consent of an instrument of the Central government. Law and order and the administration of criminal law are the exclusive subjects of the states, but laws have been made or amended to extend the jurisdiction of Central agencies over the subjects without the consent of the states. The contours of a Hindu Rashtra are becoming visible. Apart from the omnipresence of religion, a Hindu Rashtra will be a unitary form of government that will vastly empower the Central government and reduce the authority and autonomy of the states. The aspirations of the people of a state in respect of their history, language, culture, way of life and preferred model of development will be subordinated to a so-called national model. The precursors to this are one-nation-one-Aadhaar, one-nation-one-ration-card, one-nation-one-election and other 'oneness' projects that will concentrate absolute power in the Central government. A Hindu Rashtra is basically a divisive idea that will split the nation on religious and cultural lines as well as into Hindi-speaking states and non-Hindi-speaking states, especially the five southern states.

The BJP aims to win power in 2024 and form a third government under Mr Narendra Modi. The results of state elections – whether in favour of or against the BJP – will not affect the BJP's mission of capturing power at the Centre. According to many observers, the BJP's present influence over the people in the Hindi-speaking states (Rajasthan, Haryana, Uttar Pradesh, Bihar, Jharkhand, Madhya Pradesh, Chhattisgarh, Himachal Pradesh and Uttarakhand) and the Hindi-knowing states (Gujarat and Maharashtra) gives the party an edge over other political parties in a Lok Sabha election. If the BJP forms the Central government, even if it loses control over some state governments in the Hindi-speaking states, it will relentlessly pursue its agenda of creating a Hindu Rashtra. That will, above everything else, decide which way India will go in the remaining years of this century.

*

The other determining factor is the economic model that is followed in the country. Until the 1990s, the BJP did not have a clear economic philosophy. It was believed to be conservative and right of centre, but that was only a position it took against communists and socialists. The party reflected the interests of traders and businesspeople but that posture was to get financial support at the local level. The BJP had no articulated view on an open economy, delicensing, competition, free trade, etc. In fact, it was protectionist (supporting licensing and high tariffs) and its trade union wing, the Bharatiya Mazdoor Sangh, was an ardent defender of the state continuing to own enterprises. Even today, the BJP is *business*-friendly and not *market*-friendly, and it fails to understand the difference between the two. The Modi government unabashedly follows cronyism, favouring some businesspeople over others. It has not hesitated to use its agencies to help some and hurt others. Its policies support duopolies and oligopolies. It has considerably weakened the Competition Commission of India. Its relationship with the Reserve Bank of India and the Securities and Exchange Board of India is transactional; the BJP does not acknowledge their absolute independence in their respective spheres.

The BJP is satisfied with moderate growth, more than tolerable inflation and more than acceptable unemployment. I call it the 6:6:8 model – 6 per cent growth of GDP, 6 per cent rate of inflation and 8 per cent unemployment rate. This model will be disastrous for India. We may not be an impoverished country but we will not be a middle-income country either (World Bank standard: per capita income of USD 13,200 a year). Among the counties of the world, India will have the largest number of 'poor' and the largest number of undernourished children. India will also have the largest number of people not participating in the labour force and the largest number of semi-educated and unskilled workers. While a small proportion of the population will be rich and have a standard of life equal to that of the people of rich countries, a large proportion will have few assets and a small share of the national income. The only bright feature will be more public goods and of better quality but that will be offset by a deterioration in other non-economic areas such as policing, women's safety, freedom of speech, religious freedom, independence of the media, among others.

The consequences of moderate growth will be disastrous for a country with a population of 140 crore and growing until we reach, maybe, 170 crore in 2065. A low or slow rate of growth will have a negative impact on aspects such as national security, provision of public goods and services, per capita income and quality of life for the average citizen.

We have a choice: trudge slowly on the familiar path or radically reset our economic policies to accelerate growth with the goal of abolishing abject poverty (that afflicts nearly 20 per cent of the population), creating millions of regular jobs, sharply reducing inequalities in wealth and income, and ensuring a more healthy, educated and skilled people. When I say this, I believe I speak for Aspirational India. I do not believe that the BJP has the leaders or the vision to reset India's economic policies. I may also concede that other political parties have not shown sufficient interest in the reset of economic policies. It is this factor, more than any other, that will decide which way India will go in the next few decades.

*

Krishan Chopra (then with Penguin Books) had published my first collection of columns in 2004. He and Jaishree Ram Mohan, on behalf of Bloomsbury, suggested that a book of the columns during the twelve months after the 75th Independence Day (between August 2022 and August 2023), covering as they did major areas such as the economy, the law and legal matters, the challenges to democracy and politics, would be of interest to readers, as a view, albeit from an Opposition leader's perspective, on the state of the nation. Initially, I was sceptical. I decided to read the columns again and it became apparent that during that twelve-month period the Central government had made a determined attempt to steer the country in a different and, in my view, dangerous direction. The government had pressed the accelerator on the political issues and it was making every effort to assert its control over the economy. I could sense the government's desire to change the course and direction of the country. I found that in many columns written during the period I had rung the alarm bells. It made sense to put the essays together and ask readers to read them at one place and comprehend the magnitude of the challenge. Of course, there are many million Indians who may approve of the BJP-inspired course correction, but I thought it was necessary to awaken the others to the dangers of the new course. Hence, I agreed that Bloomsbury may publish the columns. I am grateful to Krishan Chopra and Jaishree Ram Mohan, who have been of great help in putting together this collection, helping decide on the title, designing the cover and publishing the book. I had little to do except reread the columns and correct the few obvious errors.

I remain grateful to the publishers and editors of the *Indian Express* for carrying my column every week for the last nearly ten years. The columns are also available on their website, www.indianexpress.com. The column is my secure way of communicating to the people of India.

I leave it to the readers to decide whether the events that happened and the actions taken during the watershed year (and in subsequent few months) will alter the course of the country for better or worse.

PART 1

Challenges to Democracy

Democracy is not a given. We cannot assume that what is true of Britain, the United States or Australia will be true for India for all time to come. The fate of countries that won independence around 1947 should alert us to what is possible. There are many reasons why I believe democracy is gasping for breath in India. There are events and developments in the last ten years that should warn us that 'eternal vigilance is the price of liberty'.

'Sovereign, Secular, Democratic'

Readers will recall the three words Sovereign, Secular and Democratic in the Preamble to the Constitution of India. They are the defining qualities of a modern republic. India won its freedom on August 15, 1947, in order to establish such a republic.

On August 15, 2022, the nation will celebrate the 75th anniversary of Independence. I am certain the nation will survive to celebrate the 100th anniversary and many more anniversaries, but – I ask this question with great trepidation – will the Republic remain sovereign, secular and democratic in 2047?

Whither Sovereignty?

For centuries, most parts of India were sovereign only in the sense they were not ruled by foreign kings and queens. The state was 'sovereign' but the people were not. Several rulers were despots, incompetent and did little to improve the lives of the people.

Under a republican Constitution, it is not only the State that is sovereign, the people are also sovereign. The power to change the rulers is the hallmark of a sovereign people. Free and fair election is the sovereign right of the people. However, in recent years, that has come under a cloud. Elections, nowadays, seem to be largely determined by money and it is the Bharatiya Janata Party (BJP) which has the largest amount of money. In fact, the BJP government invented a diabolically clever and opaque instrument (electoral bonds) to garner nearly 95 per cent of the money donated to political parties. The BJP also has other instruments to win elections: media that is tamed, institutions that are captured, laws that are weaponised and agencies that are suborned. And if the BJP loses an election, it has the ultimate weapon called Operation Lotus that it shamelessly employed in Goa, Manipur, Arunachal Pradesh, Meghalaya, Karnataka and Madhya Pradesh and attempted in Rajasthan.

Will we reach a point when elections cease to be free or fair? I sincerely hope not, but that danger cannot be ruled out altogether. Congress-mukt Bharat is not a bullet aimed at the Congress alone. Mr J.P. Nadda's statement that 'small parties will vanish leaving only the BJP as a national party' is more than the usual political rhetoric; it is an idea that is carefully nurtured in the BJP nursery.

The people will not lose their sovereignty in a flash. It will be like the spread of slow poison. The erosion will begin by depriving, bit by bit, personal liberty, freedom of speech and writing, right to dissent, right to protest, privacy, freedom to travel and, ultimately, freedom from fear. Ask yourself, in which direction is India headed?

Whither Secularism?

India will be the most populous country in a few years and the population will peak at 160 crore. Since fertility rates are converging, the religious composition of the population will not change significantly from the current proportions: Hindu 78.4 per cent, Muslim 14.4, Christian 2.2, Sikh 1.7 and others 3.3. For 2,000 years India was a plural country and, today, India is a plural country, but we seem to be in an overdrive to deny our pluralism. On the contrary, the US, Canada, Australia and New Zealand, among others, proudly acknowledge the huge benefits of having a plural society. Their institutions including courts, media and universities actively seek and promote diversity in their ranks. Currently, there is one honourable judge each from the Muslim and Christian communities in the Supreme Court and none from the Sikhs. There is an apprehension that another Muslim or Christian judge may not be appointed until after the incumbent retires.

Ask yourself, can India be anything but secular? Our music, literature, cinema, sports, science, medicine, law, teaching and civil services will be poorer if we exclude Muslims and Christians. It is the leaders of the BJP and the Rashtriya Swayamsevak Sangh (RSS) who gave a bad name to secularism. They called it 'appeasement', and that has distorted their outlook and policy on Jammu and Kashmir, electoral representation, reservations, language, food habits, clothes and personal law. The death of secularism and the declaration of a Hindu rashtra (nation) will be a body blow to the idea of India and may hasten the death of democracy itself. The overwhelming majority of Indians does not wish that outcome, but the overwhelming majority of BJP supporters seems to want a Hindu rashtra. When an irresistible force (the Hindutva believers) meets an immovable block (the moderate and tolerant Indians), I do not know which will prevail.

Whither Democracy?

Democracy is not just voting once every five years. Democracy has to be practised every day through dialogue, discussion, debate and dissent. By that standard, democracy in India is gasping for breath. There are fewer days every year on which Parliament and the legislative assemblies meet. The Sweden-based

V-Dem Institute called India an 'electoral autocracy' and lowered India's rank to 53 in the Democracy Index 2021. Each state party fights for its space in its home-state but is loath to help other state parties to protect their spaces or to join forces to fight the BJP. Nightmarish as it may seem, we cannot rule out the emergence of a virtual one-party system (as Mr Nadda devoutly wishes). His party will claim we are a democracy but with Indian characteristics!

On the occasion of the 75th anniversary of Indian Independence, when you salute the tricolour, please remember its designer, Pingali Venkayya, and that, in the current political context, the tricolour represents sovereignty, secularism and democracy.

August 14, 2022

Wish Honourable PM Will Say

Brothers and Sisters!

On this day, 75 years ago, India woke to life and freedom. In the words of Jawaharlal Nehru, our first prime minister, we made 'a tryst with destiny'. Successive governments have done their best to preserve and protect our Constitution; to defend our sovereignty and territorial integrity; to spur the growth of our economy; and to provide health, education, jobs and succour to our people. There were, indeed, aberrations and failures; but whenever we stumbled and fell, we picked ourselves up and continued our journey.

Democracy was able to correct our errors and overcome our failures. That is why we renew our pledge, on this day every year, to remain steadfast on the democratic path.

Time for Truth

I have spoken to you on eight occasions from this very spot on the ramparts of the Red Fort. I spoke as prime minister and as leader of a party. Today, I wish to strike a different note. While I speak to you as head of the government, I also wish to speak as a fellow citizen who understands and shares your sorrows, concerns, hopes and aspirations. Please bear with me while I speak the truth which, in some aspects, is quite painful.

In the last eight years, my government has made mistakes that have affected our economy. The first mistake was demonetisation. I was advised that demonetisation would eliminate black money, reduce corruption and end terrorism. I did not heed the caution of the Governor of the Reserve Bank. None of the objectives of demonetisation has been achieved. On the contrary, demonetisation set back the growth rate, caused a huge loss of jobs and, above all, led to the closure of hundreds of thousands of micro, small and medium enterprises (MSMEs).

The next mistake were the goods and services tax (GST) laws that were poorly drafted and hurriedly passed. I wish I had accepted the advice of the Chief Economic Adviser (CEA) and Opposition leaders and adopted a moderate, single rate of GST. We find ourselves trapped in a law that has vested arbitrary powers in the Central government, created grave mistrust between the Centre and states, caused huge resentment among the business and trading community, and stoked inflation. I realise that I have mounted a tiger that I cannot dismount. I intend to consult renowned economists and Opposition leaders and bring GST 2.0 replacing the present GST.

Will Withdraw from Mistakes

I made other mistakes but, after some resistance, I retraced my steps. My attempt to dilute the new Land Acquisition Act was abandoned in time. Likewise, I realised that the three farm laws were fundamentally wrong and I am happy that I repealed them. There are other mistakes which are powder kegs, such as the National Population Register (NPR), the Citizenship (Amendment) Act (CAA) and the recently announced Agnipath scheme. I assure you that I shall soon withdraw from these misadventures which are polarising the country and promoting conflict.

My fellow citizens! I make a promise that I will not yield to pressure from some quarters to restrict the scope of the Places of Worship Act or introduce a Uniform Civil Code (UCC). I promise that I shall reintroduce the Constitution

Amendment Bill to provide one-third reservation for women in Parliament and state legislatures. I also promise to issue directions to reduce the GST rates, the non-shared cesses on petrol and diesel, and the price of cooking gas.

Bridge the Divide

On past occasions, my ministers and I had made claims about various initiatives that my government had planned. I had promised to put Rs 15 lakh in the bank account of every citizen. I had promised that two crore jobs will be created every year. These were election-time jumlas. From the ramparts of the Red Fort in New Delhi, I had claimed that by 2022 the income of farmers will be doubled; that every family will have a house; and that the economy will reach the level of USD 5 trillion. I confess that these are still work-in-progress. I had also claimed that India is open defecation free (ODF) and that electricity has been provided to every home. These claims were not true. The fifth National Family Health Survey (NFHS-5) has revealed that 25.9 per cent of rural households and 6 per cent of urban households do not have access to a toilet. None of the 30 states surveyed is ODF. A survey conducted by Smart Power India and NITI Aayog in 2020 found that 13 per cent of the population was either not connected to the grid or did not use any electricity at all. I promise to consult the chief ministers and announce revised target dates to achieve these goals.

My foremost worry is the growing communal divide. No country can progress until all the people – especially women, Dalits, Muslims and tribals – feel safe and secure and are able to share the fruits of progress. I accept that my party has to shed its prejudices and my government has to do more to put an end to the divisive rhetoric finally, punish those who promote hatred, celebrate

India's diversity and pluralism, and make our government and institutions more inclusive and representative of all sections of the people.

Brothers and sisters! Our journey will be a long one. I pledge myself to the service of this great country and of all the people of India, and I appeal to you to join me on this historic journey.

JAI HIND!

August 21, 2022

My Right to Live without Fear

None could have poured out the anguish of a human better than an abused, violated and bereaved mother by the name of Bilkis Bano. In a few simple but heart-rending words she summed up the situation of millions of poor, discriminated and oppressed citizens: 'Give me back my right to live without fear.'

Killers' Sanskar

The tragic story of Ms Bilkis Bano is well documented. In 2002, following the burning of a train, violence erupted in Gujarat. Ms Bilkis Bano, 21, was a young mother and also pregnant. A mob of men attacked her, gang-raped her and killed seven members of her family including her three-year-old daughter. She was lucky to survive and tell her story. Her assailants were tried; eleven were found guilty and sentenced to imprisonment for life. Without any forewarning, on August 15, 2022, hours after the prime minister asked people to take pride in Nari Shakti, the state government remitted the remainder of the sentence of life imprisonment and the eleven prisoners walked free. They were welcomed and feted with garlands and sweets. Some in the welcoming party touched the feet of the released prisoners. One said, 'They were Brahmins with good sanskar.'

A ten-member committee had allowed the application for remission. Of the seven private members (the other three were officials of the state government), five are active members of the BJP, including two who are sitting members of the legislative assembly (MLAs). No one from the BJP apologised in 2002. No one from the BJP has apologised in 2022. Ms Bilkis Bano, along with her family, is reported to have fled her home. No one from the BJP has expressed any concern for their safety.

Absent Equality

The moral of the story is clear. Not all Indians are equal before the law or entitled to the equal protection of the laws. Not all Indians can live their lives without fear. In fact, more and more Indians are living in fear.

- Journalists live in fear. A journalist was summoned at about ten on a cold December night to rush to an OB van to read a script on routine 'breaking' news. I asked him why he did not politely decline. He said his aged parents lived with him, he had EMIs to pay on his flat and, if he had refused, he may have lost his job. Several journalists have told me that they have to 'go along' with the biases of their newspapers and channels because they feared losing their job and, under current circumstances, will not be able to find another. They have the examples of several distinguished journalists, anchors and editors before them.
- Media owners live in fear because government advertisements will mysteriously stop. Private sector advertisers will suddenly 'economise' on their advertisement budgets. The new fear is of being 'taken over'.
- Bankers live in fear. I asked a banker if his bank got many big-ticket loan requests and if he was sanctioning them. He looked around to make sure no one was

within earshot and whispered his answer: 'Why would I, sir, I will retire in six months.'

- Officers live in fear. In the first year of the Modi government, believing the yarn that the government appreciated candour, a senior officer explained at a meeting why the proposal that was being discussed was a bad idea and bad economics. He was abruptly transferred. IAS and IPS officers have found a way to avoid the ignominy: few opt for Central deputation, stumping the Central government!

Fear among Citizens

- Members of Parliament (MPs) live in fear. BJP MPs have opposed, privately, a bill or some provisions of a bill or the suspension of Opposition MPs. Recent examples are the farm bills, the Criminal Procedure (Identification) Bill and the suspension of some MPs for a whole week or for the remainder of the session.
- Ministers live in fear. Ministers have reconciled themselves to their secretaries taking instructions daily from the Prime Minister's Office (PMO) or Cabinet Secretariat and putting up files to the ministers according to those instructions. Ministers sign on Cabinet Notes drafted in the Cabinet Secretariat and submit them to the Cabinet Secretariat for submission to the Cabinet!
- Businesspersons and traders live in fear. It is no longer fear of only the Central Bureau of Investigation (CBI), Enforcement Directorate (ED) and Income Tax. Other agencies such as GST administration, DRI, SFIO, SEBI, CCI, NIA and NCB have been weaponised and unleashed. With little support from the government, MSMEs live in fear of being forced by economic circumstances to shut down forever.

- Citizens live in fear of crime, mob violence, police excesses and false cases. Especially scared are women, Muslims, Christians, Dalits, tribals, migrant workers, social activists, authors, comedians, cartoonists, film producers and publishers. Not a day passes when the talons of the state do not reach a prominent member of these sections of the people.
- Students live in fear of NEET, CUET and other centrally mandated examinations and the multiple glitches that plague them. No one knows who will be selected, what will be the criteria or when the academic year will start.
- The poor live in fear of unabated inflation, losing their jobs and soaring unemployment. Many have stopped looking for non-existent jobs. The Centre for Monitoring Indian Economy (CMIE) reported that 21 million women have dropped out of the labour force between 2017 and 2022.

I wish there was someone with authority who would reassure citizens that they can live without fear. Alas, today, there is none in India.

August 28, 2022

Supremacy or Democracy?

On Saturday, May 12, Aishwarya Thatikonda, an Indian citizen, 27, died in Allen, Texas, United States. She was visiting a mall with a friend, a usual weekend pastime. She was killed, reportedly, by Mauricio Garcia, a former security guard. Seven other persons were also killed. The killer did not know any of the eight victims and he had no motive against any of them.

Scouring the social media pages of Garcia, it was found that he was a white supremacist. The colour of the skin, white, he apparently believed, made the race superior to people of colour – black, brown, yellow or mixed – and therefore a cause to hate them. There is no scientific, evolutionary, biological, anatomical, empirical or rational explanation to support the theory that white people are superior to people of any other colour in any field. The world's best athletes are black. The world's largest bank belongs to the Chinese. The world's largest oil company belongs to the Arabs. Indians are the largest producers of cotton, milk and films.

Hark Back to Nazism

White supremacy is not a new phenomenon. The Nazis considered white Germans a superior 'master race' and they looked upon people of other races – black, Slavs, Roma, Jews and other ethnic groups – as inferior. Fascists believed in ultra-nationalism but in course of time absorbed racist ideas and became anti-Semitic. The

Nazis and the Fascists were comprehensively defeated in World War II by an alliance of forces belonging to many races.

White supremacy is not the only supremacist theory around. There is religious supremacy, casteist supremacy, linguistic supremacy and so on. India is home to every kind and sub-kind of supremacist theory. Caste and sub-caste hierarchies and casteist supremacists have prevailed for centuries until reformists such as Basaveswara, Jyotiba Phule, Narayana Guru, E.V.R. 'Periyar' Ramasamy, Babasaheb Ambedkar and others campaigned relentlessly against caste. Yet the scourge of caste grips India.

Supremacists Get Impetus

Religious supremacy has got a new lease of life thanks to the RSS, the BJP and the many Hindutva organisations. However, until the advent of the Narendra Modi government, the Indian State remained, by and large, secular. Jawaharlal Nehru, born in a patrician Brahmin family and who became India's first prime minister, preached and resolutely upheld secularism. B.R. Ambedkar, born in a Dalit family, crafted a Constitution that declared India will be a secular state.

The Constitution protected the minorities and their rights against a possible dominance or exclusion by the Hindus who were – and are – an overwhelming majority. Save a few aberrations, the State and religious institutions were separate for over sixty years. The Muslims, Christians, Sikhs, Jains, Buddhists, Parsis, Jews and non-believers, although they suffered discrimination in social life, felt safe against the power of the State. The State did not practise discrimination against religious minorities. In cases of discrimination, the judges struck down the State's action and upheld secularism. Most Hindus respected religious diversity. Political parties played by the rules.

Slide into Tribalism

All those seem to be things of the past. Secularism has become a discredited word. Many political parties seem to be vying with each other to identify themselves with one religion or another, even as their leaders profess secularism. The rapid descent into religion-based politics was witnessed in the just-concluded elections in Karnataka. A reference to the Bajrang Dal, a strongarm political outfit that indulges in hate speech and often violence, was twisted as a reference to Bajrang Bali (devotees of Lord Hanuman).

The BJP desperately tried to convert the political contest into a contest between the worshippers of Lord Hanuman and others. None other than the Honourable Prime Minister began and ended his election speeches with the slogan 'Jai Bajrang Bali'. BJP's campaign took a dangerous turn when it appealed to voters to chant 'Jai Bajrang Bali' before they cast their votes. This was an egregious violation of the election laws and a supine Election Commission did absolutely nothing about it.

Karnataka's population has 12.92 per cent Muslims and 1.87 per cent Christians (Census 2011). Snubbing them, the BJP did not field a Muslim or Christian candidate in any of the 224 constituencies. BJP's leaders openly said 'we do not want the votes of Muslims'. The unstated theme of its campaign was 'Hate non-Hindu, vote Hindu'.

Mr Satyapal Singh Baghel, a minister in the Union government, captured the unarticulated views of BJP cadres when he said, 'Tolerant Muslims can be counted on fingers … Even that is a tactic. People keep talking about the Constitution's basic structure and how it cannot be tinkered with. The basic structure of this nation is that of Akhand Bharat Hindu Rashtra before 1192.' And he is the country's minister for law and justice!

As far as I know, not once has the leadership of the BJP condemned the lynching of Muslims, the vandalising of Christian churches, the threats to young couples or the violence unleashed by vigilante groups. Religious supremacists are on the rampage. Karnataka's voters have the first opportunity to stop the dangerous slide into tribalism and save democracy from religious supremacists.

When you read this essay you will get a clue to what the future holds.

May 14, 2023

Rebuff to Centralism

It is said that 'misfortunes don't come singly'. The week beginning May 7, 2023, was brutal for the BJP. On May 11, the Supreme Court delivered two judgements. Both were of Constitution Benches (five judges) and both interpreted key provisions of the Constitution. Both amounted to two tight slaps on the face of the government. The Karnataka election results came on May 13.

The BJP government's refuge in the case of adversity is 'silence'. Neither the usually self-assured Hon'ble Home Minister nor the voluble former Hon'ble Law Minister reacted to the judgements or the Karnataka election results.

Constitutional Transgressions

The Delhi case was quite simple. In 2018, the Supreme Court had interpreted Article 239AA of the Constitution and held that in all matters save public order, police and land, the executive power was vested in the council of ministers of the Delhi government and the Lieutenant Governor (LG), Delhi was obliged to act on the 'aid and advice' of the council of ministers. There was lingering doubt about 'services' – who will control the civil servants. The issue was put to rest by the May 11 judgement and it was declared that the ministers had control over the 'services'. Every LG since 2014 must share the blame for not honouring the essence of a democratic, federal system of government.

The second case was complex only because the provisions of the Tenth Schedule of the Constitution had not been interpreted authoritatively and unambiguously in previous judgements. After the Tenth Schedule was amended in 2004 there is no concept of a 'split' in a legislature party. The Tenth Schedule allowed an exception from the perils of defection only if one of two conditions was satisfied: (1) if the parent political party merged with another political party and not less than two-thirds of the members of the legislature party agreed to such merger; (2) if the legislator(s) has/have not accepted the merger and opted to function as a separate group in the legislature. If neither of the two conditions was satisfied, the dissident legislators continued to belong to the legislature party and were obliged to obey the whip of the parent political party.

Unconstitutional Government

A situation arose in Maharashtra where sixteen legislators led by Mr Eknath Shinde broke away from the Shiv Sena legislature party. Their parent political party had not, on that day, merged with another political party (and has not done so even today). None of the exceptional circumstances under the Tenth Schedule existed. Hence, the dissidents were obliged to act and vote as directed by the whip of Shiv Sena issued on June 21, 2022.

Defying the whip, the Eknath Shinde group joined hands with the BJP. The Governor, without any cause (as found by the Supreme Court), asked Mr Uddhav Thackeray, chief minister, to seek the vote of confidence of the legislative assembly. Mr Thackeray (on poor advice) resigned without facing the legislative assembly. Promptly, the Governor appointed Mr Shinde as the chief minister and swore in a coalition government of the Shinde group and the BJP. The Shiv Sena pressed the Speaker to disqualify the sixteen legislators. The Speaker sat on the petition (which has become the practice in many legislatures).

The Supreme Court ruled that the 'Whip' is the person appointed by the political party (in this case, Shiv Sena); that the Governor had no cause to call a session of the legislative assembly and direct Mr Thackeray to secure a vote of confidence; and that the Speaker was obliged to decide on the disqualification petition as soon as possible.

In this essay, I am concerned with the conduct of the constitutional functionaries. It is clear that the Governor *exceeded* his jurisdiction and the Speaker *did not exercise* his jurisdiction. Both were guilty of dereliction of duty. Both were complicit in installing or allowing an unconstitutional government to remain in office since June 2022.

The Overarching Goal

The infamous Operation Lotus(es) in different states; the bulldozer justice in Uttar Pradesh, Madhya Pradesh and Assam; the denial or reduction of funds to non-BJP-ruled states on one pretext or other; the rash of criminal cases against Opposition political leaders; the constitutionally suspect laws such as the amendment of Article 370 and the law on electoral bonds; the threat of enacting a Uniform Civil Code; the threat of creating a National Register of Citizens; the use of List III-Concurrent List to override state laws (for example, on education); the usurpation of taxation powers under the GST laws; and many other actions are aimed at achieving one overarching goal – to bring 140 crore people under one umbrella of governance under an omnipotent and omnipresent Central government.

It is called 'centralism'. Examples of countries where 'centralism' prevails are China, Russia, Turkey, etc.

The two judgements of the Supreme Court have interdicted the drift towards 'centralism'. The Karnataka verdict has derailed the vaunted double-engine government. The best inoculation against 'centralism' is to keep our electoral and political system *plural* – several parties winning power in the states and at least two parties contesting for power at the Centre. Two battles have been won in the Supreme Court and one in Karnataka, but many more lie ahead.

May 21, 2023

Sengol That Must Not Bend

Tiruvalluvar, Elango Adigal, Avvaiyyar and the Sangam poets will turn in their graves if they heard about the startling interpretation of Sengol by the Honourable Prime Minister, the distorians and the BJP's spin doctors. In their interpretation, Sengol has become the symbol of temporal power. The imaginary handing over of the Sengol by a priest or a former ruler to the new ruler has been portrayed as a transfer of power.

How history and an ethical principle can be shamelessly distorted was demonstrated on May 28, 2023. The trumpeters played the trumpets, the courtiers fawned on the ruler and the inauguration of a new building that will accommodate the two Houses of Parliament was converted into a virtual coronation. Lord Mountbatten and C. Rajagopalachari (Rajaji) were summoned to be witnesses to a royal ceremony that was incongruous in a democratic republic. It was unfortunate that self-effacing heads of Saivite adheenams (mutts) were called to inject a large dose of religiosity into what ought to have been a secular event.

As the people watched the proceedings on their television screens, they would have surely contrasted the choreographed ritual with the unadorned swearing-in of President Murmu on July 25, 2022. And the people, especially of Karnataka, would have wondered 'who was transferring power to whom?'

Poet Defined Sengol

In 31 BCE, Tiruvalluvar, a Tamil poet and philosopher, wrote his immortal verses that are contained in the celebrated *Tirukkural*. In the part called Wealth, he included two chapters titled 'Sengonmai' (Righteous Sceptre) and 'Kodungonmai' (Cruel Sceptre). Couplet 546 reads:

> Velandri vendri tharuvathu mannavan Kol aduoom kodathu enin

Kol is the sceptre. The verse means that 'it is not the spear that brings victory to the ruler, it is the Kol [sceptre]', but mark the poet's last three words: the *Kol that will not bend.* The sceptre must be erect. It must not bend this way or that. The same thought is present in the oath taken by the prime minister on being sworn in '… I will do right to all manner of people in accordance with the Constitution and the laws without fear or favour, affection or ill-will'. The Kol is a symbol of righteous rule, no more, no less. It will be a Sengol if it did not bend, if it bends it will be a cruel rule.

Sengol stands for righteous rule, not power. The ruler who holds the sceptre promises to govern righteously. Tiruvalluvar placed the Sengol as one among four virtues of the ruler: 'Charity, compassion, righteous rule and protection of the weak (poor) are the four virtues of a good king' (Kural 390). Another chapter is titled 'Kodungonmai', the opposite of Sengonmai, and described as cruel or unjust rule.

Songs Praising Sengol

A Sangam poet praised Karikalan, the legendary Chola king, for his 'aranodu punarnda tiranari Sengol', meaning that his wise rule was wedded to ethics. Another Sangam poet described the ruler as 'Erorku nizhandra kolin', meaning that the ruler ensured that the farmers who produced food faced no distress. Elango Adigal, a Jain monk, who authored the epic *Silappathikaram*, bemoaned the injustice done to Kannagi and prophesied the doom of the king who had caused the Sengol to bend.

Avvaiyyar, a people's poet, composed verses in simple language. A celebrated poem reads:

> When the bund rises, water will rise,
> when water rises, paddy will rise,
> when paddy rises, families will rise,
> when families rise, the kol (sceptre) will rise,
> and when the sceptre rises erect, the ruler will rise

A sceptre that will bend is the mark of an unjust or cruel rule. There cannot be any bias towards one section or bias against another. There is no place for ill will against any community or religion or language.

To give contemporary examples, there can be no place for hate speeches or vigilantism or love jihad or bulldozer justice. There can be no place for the Citizenship (Amendment) Act that discriminates against Muslims of any neighbouring country, Christians and Buddhists of Nepal, and Tamils of Sri Lanka. There can be no place for 'farm laws' that put farmers at the mercy of traders and monopolists. There can be no place for snatching a project from Maharashtra and taking it to Gujarat. A righteous ruler's political party cannot refuse to field a candidate from the Muslim or Christian community in a state election like the just-concluded election in Karnataka. Nor can a righteous ruler's police break, by use of force, a peaceful protest by medal-winning sportspersons who sought justice.

Don't Defile Sengol

To equate the sceptre with power is to defile the concept of Sengol. To cite Lord Mountbatten and Rajaji is not only to distort history but belittle a pragmatic viceroy and a wise scholar-statesman and attribute to them a lack of common sense.

Let the Sengol adorn the podium where the Speaker will sit. Let it be a silent witness to the proceedings of the House. The Sengol will stand upright if there is free debate in the House; if there is full play for freedom of speech and expression; if there is the freedom to disagree and to dissent; and if there is the freedom to vote against unjust or unconstitutional laws. Let us hope the Sengol and what it stands for – Sengonmai (Righteous Rule) – will prevail.

June 4, 2023

Discovering Democracy in America

Althing, 48 kilometres east of Reykjavik, Iceland, is believed to be the seat of the oldest parliament in the world (c. 930). Iceland is rich, but humble, and is a democratic country. Not all countries with a parliament are democracies. Examples of this kind are well known.

India has a parliament but there are, increasingly, questions whether India is truly a democracy. It was therefore reassuring to hear the Honourable Prime Minister declare on his recent visit to the United States that India 'is a democracy'. He uttered the word 'democracy' fourteen times in his address to the joint session of the US Congress. News reports say that he 'pushed back' at a question on minority rights and free speech from a reporter at the White House.

Ms Sabrina Siddique, a *Wall Street Journal* reporter, was lucky that she was allowed to ask a question – a privilege that has been denied to journalists in India during the last nine years. The prime minister's answer (as translated) was surprisingly long and detailed:

Q: …what steps are you and your government willing to take to improve the rights of Muslims and other minorities in your country and uphold free speech?

A: I'm actually really surprised that people say so. And so, people don't say it. Indeed, India is a democracy.

And the prime minister asserted, 'There is no question of discrimination on the ground of caste and religion.'

There are 203 million Muslims (14.2 per cent of the population), 33 million Christians (2.3 per cent), 24 million Sikhs (1.7 per cent) and other minorities in India. Are they discriminated against is a question that must be put to them. Here are some facts that will help you find an answer:

On Religious Discrimination

- In the 79-strong council of ministers, there is no Muslim, one Christian and one Sikh, though the BJP has 395 MPs in the Lok Sabha and the Rajya Sabha.
- The BJP fielded only six Muslim candidates in the Lok Sabha election in 2019 – three in Jammu and Kashmir, two in West Bengal and one in Lakshadweep – and all of them lost.
- Consequently, Muslims constitute only 4.42 per cent of the strength of the Lok Sabha, though Muslims constitute about 14.2 per cent of the population.
- In the last elections to the respective state assemblies in Uttar Pradesh (403 seats), Gujarat (182) and Karnataka (224), the BJP did not field a single Muslim candidate in the three states.
- Of the thirty-four judges of the Supreme Court, currently, there is one Muslim, one Parsi and no Christian or Sikh. The whisper is 'one is representative enough'.
- In May 2019, Jammu and Kashmir, the only Muslim-majority state in India, was dismembered and its status was reduced to a Union Territory.
- The Citizenship (Amendment) Act is discriminatory against Muslims from neighbouring countries. It also excludes migrants who are Buddhists and Christians from Nepal and migrants of any religion from Sri Lanka and Myanmar.
- Controversies were ignited on hijab, halal, azaan and prayers by Muslims on public grounds on the eve of

the elections in Karnataka by the BJP and its fraternal organisations.

- Cow protection and love jihad are campaigns supported by the BJP that have the effect of targeting Muslim dairy-owners and traders and Muslim youth.
- There were 2,900 incidents of violence between religious communities between 2017 and 2021, according to the National Crime Records Bureau (NCRB). Twenty-eight persons were killed in 'lynching' between 2010 and 2017 (twenty-four were Muslims). In 2017, NCRB stopped collecting data on lynching.
- According to a special report in *Outlook* (March 13, 2023), Christians in India continue to face targeted attacks on their faith, including threats to Christian gatherings, churches and educational institutions.
- The US Report on International Religious Freedom, 2022 (May 15, 2023) said that religious freedom in India had worsened. The 49-page report cited examples of cases where minorities were targeted and attacked.
- India's rank slipped from 100 in 2022 to 108 in 2023 in the Electoral Democracy Index of Norway's V-Dem Institute. It described India as an 'electoral autocracy'.
- US-based Freedom House downgraded India's status to 'partially free' in its Freedom in the World report.

On Freedom of Speech

- In December 2022, there were seven journalists in jail; of them five were Muslims. Two were released on bail after fourteen months (Mr Manan Dar) and two years (Mr Siddique Kappan), respectively.
- People have been arrested for criticising the prime minister and chief ministers. Example: five men were

arrested for the crime of putting up a hoarding that showed Mr Modi offering a cooking gas cylinder priced at Rs 1,105.

- Mr Mohammad Zubair, co-founder of Alt News, a fact-checking website, was arrested on a complaint by a person who alleged that Mr Zubair had called some Hindu monks 'hatemongers' and had hurt his religious sentiments. New charges were added for old tweets. Finally, the Supreme Court consolidated the FIRs and granted Mr Zubair bail in all cases including future FIRs.
- According to Access Now, an international digital rights organisation, the world saw 187 shutdowns of the Internet in 2022. India accounted for 84.
- In the World Press Freedom Index 2023, India slid to rank 161 out of 180 countries.

I wish the prime minister will answer questions of journalists in India on religious discrimination and freedom of speech.

July 2, 2023

Legislating Authoritarianism

Authoritarianism is the antithesis of government according to law. Under authoritarianism, there is reduction in the rule of law, rejection of plurality, centralisation of power and imposition of the will of the majority or, sometimes, one person. Authoritarianism is usually associated with rubber-stamp parliaments where all or nearly all seats are held by the ruling dispensation. Such parliaments too pass laws!

Unfortunately, democratically elected parliaments have begun to copy authoritarian parliaments. And pass laws that may or may not pass the test of legality. Such laws, in my view, certainly do not pass the test of legitimacy. A recent example of a legislation lacking in legitimacy is the bill passed by Israel's parliament (the Knesset) restricting the power of the courts to review the validity of laws made by parliament.

What Is Constitutional?

India is not far behind. (Since fingers will be pointed to the Constitution Amendments and legislation passed during the Emergency [June 25, 1975 to March 21, 1977], let me straightaway admit that many of the amendments made and laws passed did not satisfy the test of either legality or legitimacy.) That shop-worn argument out of the way, let's look at examples of recent legislation that were passed by the Parliament of India.

The government takes a narrow view of 'constitutionality' – that the law should not contravene any express provision of the Constitution. But as the Supreme Court has pointed out there are implicit boundaries that shall not be crossed: for example, constitutional morality and proportionality. Another boundary has been pointed out by Mr Suhrith Parthasarathy (*The Hindu*, dated August 1, 2023), who opined that 'the Indian Constitution brims with moral values' and framed the boundary as 'the sanctity attached to the various subtleties' in the relationship between the Union and the states. In the current monsoon session, there are at least three bills that crossed the constitutional boundaries:

The Forest (Conservation) Amendment Bill

Between 2001 and 2021, the total forest cover increased from 675,538 square kilometres to 713,789 square kilometres, mostly land with tree canopy density of 10–40 per cent. (The decline in forest cover with canopy density above 40 per cent was only 37,251 square kilometres.) The Amendment Bill reverses the gains of forty years by introducing retrograde provisions. Land recorded as forest but not notified before October 25, 1980 and land diverted to non-forest use before December 12, 1996 will be excluded. Non-notified natural forests ('deemed forests') will be excluded. These exclusions are contrary to the judgement of the Supreme Court in the *T.N. Godavarman* case, the Forest Rights Act, 2006 and the judgement in the *Niyamgiri Hills* case. Land situated within 100 kilometres from international borders for linear projects for national security will be excluded. Almost the whole of many north-eastern states and the Himalayan region, which have the highest forest cover and are biodiversity hotspots, fall within the said

100 kilometres. Land for strategic and security-related infrastructure will be excluded. The list of non-forest purposes has been trimmed; zoos, safaris, ecotourism will no longer be non-forest purposes; and any land may be excluded from non-forest purposes under terms and conditions specified by the Central government.

More than the drastic dilution of the Forest (Conservation) Act, 1980, the manner in which the amendments were made reveals authoritarianism. The bill was not referred to the Standing Committee concerned but to a Joint Parliamentary Committee (JPC). The JPC, by a majority, recommended no changes. Six Opposition MPs recorded a powerful dissent. Without further consultation, and brushing aside the objections of forest dwellers, experts, environmentalists and civil society organisations, the bill was pushed through without a meaningful debate.

The Multi-state Cooperative Societies (Amendment) Bill

A Central government–appointed Election Authority will conduct elections to Multi-state cooperative societies. Government's shareholding in such societies cannot be redeemed without prior approval, ensuring government's perpetual presence and control. Complaints of members will be adjudicated by Central government–appointed ombudsmen. Boards of multi-state cooperative societies, in which the government has a shareholding or to which government has extended a loan, may be superseded. The bill was passed amid disruption without a meaningful debate. We have bid goodbye to the hallowed principles of cooperation, namely, democracy, autonomy, self-help and absence of any government control.

The GNCTD (Amendment) Bill

Article 239 AA makes special provisions with respect to Delhi. Sub-article (4) contains the historical words 'with the Chief Minister at the head to aid and advise the Lieutenant Governor'. There can be no doubt that the Constitution envisaged a representative and parliamentary form of government for Delhi. The present government had tried every trick up its sleeve to reduce the Government of National Capital Territory of Delhi (GNCTD) to a municipality or less. It failed twice. Now the government has brought a bill that will take away control of the 'services' (meaning government officers) from the ministers and place them under the LG. The ministers will be reduced to showpieces at the mercy of the LG and his officers. The Supreme Court will decide whether the ordinance/bill is legal or not, but I am clear that it is not legitimate. The bill makes the LG appointed by the Central government a viceroy, a post that was abolished when the British were leaving India.

The three bills are examples of using parliamentary legislation to impose a centralised and authoritarian model of government. They are excesses that must be undone in the future.

August 6, 2023

Aid and Advise

The people of the National Capital Territory – in short, Delhi – are entitled to representative government. In 1992, Parliament granted them their wish and inserted Article 239AA in the Constitution of India. Since then, there have been elections held periodically to the Government of National Capital Territory of Delhi.

The BJP won the first election, the Congress the next three. The BJP's chief ministers, Madan Lal Khurana, Sahib Singh Verma and Sushma Swaraj (1993–98), and the Congress's chief minister, Sheila Dikshit (1998–2013), had no difficulty working with different Lieutenant Governors (LGs) under Article 239AA.

Asserting Control

Keeping an eye on the Lok Sabha election of 2014, and to score points over the Congress and the newly formed Aam Aadmi Party (AAP), the BJP promised full statehood for Delhi in the assembly election of 2013. It lost to the AAP. Elected to power in 2014, the BJP decided to exercise control over the GNCTD. However, the Supreme Court rejected the government's interpretation of Article 239AA and laid down the law, once again, that real power vested in the council of ministers and not with the LG (2018).

Not one to give up so easily, the BJP persisted with the argument that control over 'services' vested in the LG. On May 11, 2023, the Supreme Court reaffirmed its view and held that GNCTD had legislative and executive power over 'services'. Within days of the judgement, the Central government promulgated an ordinance to take control of the 'services'. In the monsoon session of Parliament, government replaced the ordinance by legislation and passed it in both Houses.

The debate on the Delhi Bill was on expected lines. The BJP interpreted 'constitutionality' in a narrow manner and said that the bill did not violate any provision of the Constitution. The Opposition argued that the bill was unconstitutional on several grounds. It is wise to leave the last word to the Supreme Court.

Westminster Model

In my view, the debate in Parliament missed the wood for the trees. The desired model of a government could vary from military dictatorship (latest example, Niger) to one-party dictatorship (China) to presidential government (United States) to presidential-cum-parliamentary government (France) to multiparty government (many countries of Europe) to elected autocracy (Hungary) to pure parliamentary democracy (United Kingdom). What did India choose when the Constitution was adopted? Unambiguously, it was parliamentary democracy of the Westminster model.

The foundations of parliamentary democracy are an elected House of the People, members of Parliament representing singular constituencies, a council of ministers with the prime minister (or the chief minister) at the head answerable to Parliament (or the assembly) and the Parliament answerable to the people. Other constitutional bodies are created by the Constitution – for example, the Supreme Court, the Election Commission, the Public Service Commission, etc. The civil service is constituted by the government according to need. Civil servants are appointed and answerable to the ministers of the government.

What is the role of the President or the Governor? He or she occupying the office is the Head of the State (HoS). The HoS is the symbol of formal authority but enjoys no actual power which vests in the council of ministers.

The Law Declared

The question will arise, does the Constitution say that the ministers hold actual power and the HoS is only the symbol of formal authority? The answer is yes and lies in the three magical words 'aid and advise'. These words have a special meaning in constitutional legal history. Aid does not mean running to the help of another person; advise does not mean offering solicited or unsolicited counsel. Aid and advise is the essence of parliamentary democracy.

The magical words are in Articles 74, 163 and 239AA of the Constitution in the context of the roles of the prime minister and the president, the chief minister and the governor, and the chief minister of GNCTD and the LG, respectively. Babasaheb Ambedkar, explaining the meaning of the words, said, 'The President … can do nothing contrary to their advice nor can he do anything without their advice.' Justice Krishna Iyer pronounced: 'We declare the law of this branch of our Constitution to be that the President and Governor … shall … exercise their formal constitutional powers only upon and in accordance with the advice of their Ministers save in a few well-known exceptional situations.'

The bill passed by Parliament turned parliamentary democracy on its head. A three-member Civil Service Authority consisting of the chief minister, chief secretary and home secretary (the last two appointed by the LG) will be vested with control of all aspects relating to government servants. The home secretary will convene the meetings and two members will constitute the quorum. Decisions will be taken by a majority. Even unanimous decisions of the Civil Service Authority can be overturned by the LG. The inevitable result will be that the chief minister, in a parody of the famous television serial, may only say, 'Yes, secretary'! The apt name for the bill would have been Government of National Capital Territory of Delhi (Appointment of Viceroy) Bill, 2023.

The 3,29,41,309 people of Delhi (2023) witnessed the deadly blows to parliamentary democracy in GNCTD. As the gravely injured parliamentary democracy is wheeled into the emergency ward, the people of Delhi will fervently pray that the victim will be saved by the Supreme Court.

August 13, 2023

The Future: With Hope or Fear?

On August 15, the Honourable Prime Minister spoke about the end of a thousand years of slavery and the start of a thousand years of glory. Apparently, the two millennia met at the very spot on which he was standing and at the very moment that he was speaking. If it were true, the speech would be as epoch-making as few events before – the enlightenment of Siddhartha, the birth of Jesus and the revelations to Prophet Muhammad. Or, in material terms, as epoch-making as the falling of the apple, the discovery of electricity, the invention of the telephone, the flight of the Wright Flyer, the splitting of the atom or the landing on the moon. I was sorry that I was not a witness.

I was, however, witness to a mundane, everyday event. Mr Rajdeep Sardesai, on his show on India Today, brought, face-to-face, two members of Parliament – Mr Jayant Sinha (BJP) and Mr Shashi Tharoor (Congress) – and asked them searching questions before an audience of knowledgeable and articulate college students.

The opening statements of the two guests about 'India at 100' aroused my curiosity. Mr Jayant Sinha wished for sustainable prosperity by 2047 and Mr Shashi Tharoor wished for an inclusive India by 2047. It raised a question in my mind: why can't we have both? Listening to the two parliamentarians, claiming to reflect their respective party's position, I was left with the agonising thought that, perhaps, India cannot have both.

Glaring Contrast

In this essay, I wish to explore Mr Sinha's vow to protect and preserve the Constitution of India; his full-throated support of secularism, federalism and protection of human rights, and his promise to uphold the rule of law and enforce accountability. To the moderator's direct questions, Mr Sinha answered, unequivocally, 'Yes, you have the right to marry, you have the right to eat, and you have the right to religion.' Without batting an eyelid, he asserted that 'within my party, we can express our differences. Absolutely. I have met with the senior leadership of my party and discussed matters of concern.' And to a question on what would be most important to him in 2047, Mr Sinha declared, 'Freedom and liberty.' I think Mr Sinha genuinely believes in what he said on the Rajdeep Sardesai–anchored show.

On the next day – our seventy-seventh Independence Day – the Honourable Prime Minister spoke for 90 minutes. I read the English translation of the speech. In sum, it was an 'I, me and my' speech, a medley of thoughts and a recital of what he believed had been accomplished in the last nine to ten years – until he spoke in the now-familiar coded language and railed against corruption, dynasty and appeasement. We know who his targets are. They are Opposition leaders, the Gandhi family and Muslims, respectively. At that point, the speech became a rehearsal for an election rally. Evidently, nothing has changed in the last nine to ten years.

Let's return to Mr Sinha's statements and juxtapose them with the speech of the Honourable Prime Minister. Mr Sinha was reassuring young college students that the centenary year 2047 would be a golden period. But the Honourable Prime Minister, while describing the new millennium, did not allude to any of the things that

Mr Sinha promised – not the protection or preservation of the Constitution; not secularism or federalism or protection of human rights; not upholding the rule of law; and not enforcing accountability. There was not a word on any of the millennium assurances held out by Mr Sinha. Obviously, Mr Sinha and the Honourable Prime Minister were painting different pictures of the millennium that 'started' on August 15, 2023.

Inconvenient Questions

Now, let's place Mr Sinha's statements alongside what is reported every day in the newspapers, on television channels and social media. If the young college student has the right to marry anyone of choice, why are inter-caste and interfaith couples harassed, beaten or lynched? If the young college student has the right to eat any food, what was the controversy kicked up in Karnataka about 'halal' and 'non-halal' meat? If the young college student has the right to practise any religion, what is the role of the Bajrang Dal, the Hindu mahapanchayats and the right-wing outfits and why are there hate speeches against Muslims and Christians? Above all, why is there so much violence around us?

If the promise of upholding the rule of law is true, why were there riots in Delhi, civil war in Manipur and communal violence in Nuh, Haryana? Why are bulldozers used to raze the dwellings and petty shops of the poor? If the assurance that the Constitution will be protected and preserved is true, why were laws made in Parliament to repeal Article 370, dismember the state of Jammu and Kashmir and alter the constitutional balance between the Lieutenant Governor and the elected government in Delhi?

These are inconvenient questions but, I am sure, the gathering of college students wanted answers to these questions. The two questions they were allowed to ask were probing and provocative but elicited unsatisfactory answers in an otherwise splendid show.

Sidelined Hope

I believe Mr Sinha and a few others in the BJP are secular, liberal and wish to uphold the present Constitution. Unfortunately, the leadership of their party sidelined them long ago. The grandiloquent declaration of the start of a new millennium arouses not hope but fear.

August 20, 2023

How We 'Work' the Constitution

One of the oldest democracies in the world has a sovereign (king or queen) but not a written constitution, yet it is considered a model for other constitutional democracies. Britain's governance according to the 'constitution' is superior to that of countries that have a written constitution. Contrast countries like Denmark, Sweden, Norway, Switzerland, etc. on the one hand and countries like China, Iran, Myanmar, etc. on the other. The V-Dem Institute placed the countries first mentioned at the top of the list of liberal democracies and the countries mentioned later were classified as closed autocracies.

I think India falls in between. It has a written Constitution, a long one. Dr Ambedkar, his colleagues in the Drafting Committee and the Constituent Assembly took two years, eleven months and seventeen days to complete the draft and adopt the Constitution. The Constituent Assembly debates are a model of democratic debate, dissent and decision-making.

We Stumbled, Recovered

We have worked the Constitution for seventy-three years. When Parliament found shortcomings – and sometimes even when it did not – it amended the Constitution. There have been 105 Constitution Amendment Acts so far. Many legal scholars believe that the Constitution faced an overt and grave challenge when the Emergency was in force. There have been other instances when the

Constitution faced covert challenges: the Constitution was dented, but it survived. When such occasions involved the Supreme Court of India, the Court may have stumbled, but recovered in due course. The Court proved that it possessed the humility to admit it was wrong. Examples when the Court stumbled are *A.K. Gopalan, I.C. Golak Nath* and *ADM Jabalpur*. Examples when the Court corrected itself and asserted the fundamental principles of a liberal democratic Constitution are *Maneka Gandhi*, *S.R. Bommai*, *Kesavananda Bharati* and *K.S. Puttaswamy*.

Covert Assault

Some recent events have caused concern. In my view, they are covert assaults on the Constitution.

On August 5, 2019, among other steps whose legality has been questioned, the state of Jammu and Kashmir was dismembered and two union territories were created. In a bizarre interpretation of the Constitution, Parliament consulted Parliament and after 'obtaining' the latter's 'views', Parliament reduced the state to two union territories. There is no guarantee that it will not happen to any other state in the future.

On two occasions, the Central government passed laws intended to deprive the Union Territory of Delhi (GNCTD) of the powers that it had enjoyed since 1992. On both occasions, the Supreme Court rebuffed the Central government. In the monsoon session of Parliament, government enacted a law taking away the control of the elected ministers over government employees and vesting the control in the appointed Lieutenant Governor. The ministers have been placed at the mercy of the civil servants and the LG.

The Election Commission of India (ECI) is a constitutional body vested with vast powers. It holds the key to free and fair elections and to the renewal of our commitment to democracy every five years. In *Anoop Baranwal*, the Supreme Court created a mechanism that would ensure that a non-partisan body (prime minister, Chief Justice of India and leader of the Opposition) selected the election commissioners. In a crude move, the Central government set the judgement at nought and passed a law replacing the chief justice of India by a minister nominated by the prime minister. If the law will survive a legal challenge, it could alter the course of democracy in India.

State legislatures pass bills. Under Article 200 of the Constitution, the Governor may give assent to a bill or withhold assent or reserve it for the consideration of the President. Some Governors do none of the above; they simply sit on the bills. Likewise, on proposals to nominate persons to the legislative council, Governors sit on them. On petitions for disqualification of a member for violating the Tenth Schedule of the Constitution, Speakers sit on the cases without deciding them. Does sitting on bills or cases without exercising powers amount to working the Constitution?

The latest assault on the Constitution is the situation in Manipur. The state has suffered a de facto division. No Kuki can enter the Imphal valley and no Meitei can enter the Kuki-dominated districts. The chief minister and his ministers cannot venture out of the neighbourhood of their residences. After stalling initially, the Governor has summoned the legislative assembly to meet at Imphal, but the ten Kuki members (out of sixty members) may not be able to attend the session. If this situation is not a 'breakdown' of the Constitution (and the chief minister is allowed to continue in office), Article 356 deserves to be erased from the Constitution.

Ambedkar's Caution

On November 25, 1949, Dr B.R. Ambedkar made his closing speech before the voting on the next day. He said, 'However good a Constitution may be, it is sure to turn out to be bad because those who are called to work it, happen to be a bad lot. However bad a Constitution may be, it may turn out to be good if those who are called to work it, happen to be a good lot. The working of the Constitution does not depend wholly upon the nature of the Constitution.'

Please ask yourself, are we working the Constitution or wrecking the Constitution?

August 27, 2023

PART 2

Muddled Economy

This was my favourite subject and I had written eighteen essays in the watershed year. I questioned the interpretation of official data. I cited data from reliable sources. I referred to questions I had asked in Parliament to which I got no answers. I pointed out the consequences of a slower growth rate. I flagged price rise, unemployment and the widening inequalities as the topmost concerns of the people. I believe that, eventually, economics will trump all other issues.

The Speech That I Might Have Made

Mr Chairman,

This debate should have been held several days ago. I fail to understand the difference, in substance, between a discussion under Rule 267 and any other rule. The government was stubborn, the people attributed it to its hauteur.

Let's debate price rise. This is not a debate on the state of the economy. If it were, we may have a hundred things to say about the economic management – rather, mismanagement – of this government since the day of the infamous demonetisation.

Prices are rising. Rising prices are badly hurting the people, especially the poor and the middle class. Consumption and savings have fallen, household debt has risen and malnutrition (especially among women and children) has increased. Sadly, the government is not willing to acknowledge these facts. Yesterday, I was horrified to hear the Hon'ble Finance Minister tell the other House that the increases in the GST rates did not affect the people! That statement can be put to a simple test which I shall reveal at the end of my intervention.

Causes and Course

I hope the debate in this House does not meander into by-lanes and alleys. A *tu-tu main-main* debate takes us nowhere. I urge the government and all Hon'ble Members to accept the reality of intolerable price increase and ask the only relevant question: 'What steps will the government take to contain inflation?'

The starting point is identifying the causes of the current inflation.

Let me begin with the Fiscal Deficit (FD). We know that a large and growing Fiscal Deficit affects prices. I don't have the time to explain how. In the Budget for this year, the government estimated a Fiscal Deficit of 6.4 per cent or Rs 16,61,196 crore. In April–June, the Fiscal Deficit touched Rs 3,51,871 crore. We know the government has underestimated expenditure and has not budgeted for the same. Has the government underestimated revenues too? Will the government be able to contain the Fiscal Deficit at 6.4 per cent? We want a specific answer.

More Man-made Causes

Next is the Current Account Deficit (CAD). The CAD may be near USD 30 billion in April–June. The trade deficit in July was USD 31 billion. If CAD crossed USD 100 billion for the whole year, as estimated, it would have disastrous consequences. Let the government tell this House what it proposes to do about the CAD. Again, Mr Chairman, I want a specific answer.

The third red light is the Interest Rate. We know that the policy rate is set by the Reserve Bank of India (RBI). The government has nominated three members to the Monetary Policy Committee. The government's secretary is on the RBI board. So the government cannot plead it has no responsibility. India followed the advanced economies when they pursued an accommodative monetary policy and pumped liquidity into the market. They are now increasing interest rates. I doubt if the country can take a different line now. If RBI hikes the interest rate, it may contain demand and, consequently, moderate prices, but it will also affect sales, profits and, above all, employment. The trick lies in 'calibration'. Are the government and the RBI Governor on the same page? Will the government share with us its forecast on interest rates?

The fourth is the Supply Side. Since liberal imports are ruled out for the time being, what steps will the government take to increase domestic production and supply? MSMEs are in deep distress, and they cannot help unless they are helped first. Large companies are interested in maximising profits and hence they may keep supply artificially constrained. Trade is shackled by the GST laws and rates. My question is, what does the government intend to do to ensure abundant supply of goods and services?

Original Sin

Last on my list is the item that has troubled the people the most: the government's tax policy. I charge the government with committing the original sin that fuelled inflation, namely, imposing cruel taxes and cesses on petrol and diesel. The government collected a whopping Rs 26,00,000 crore through the oil companies as taxes, cesses and dividends. This government is callous, heartless and anti-poor. Add to that the periodic hikes in GST rates on goods and services consumed by the poor and the middle class. This government does not feel the pain of six-year-old Kriti Dubey who could not understand why her mother scolded her when she asked for another pencil or the pain of the mother who cannot afford another pencil for her daughter. If this government has a head and a heart, it will immediately moderate the taxes on petrol and diesel, reduce the price of LPG, and reverse the hike in taxes on essential goods that are consumed by the poor and the middle class.

Mr Chairman, let me close with an offer of the 'test' that I alluded to earlier. Let the three of us – you Mr Chairman, the Hon'ble Finance Minister and I – drive in an unmarked car, without any security, to a middle-class neighbourhood or a slum in Delhi. Mr Chairman, please ask the people if they are affected by the fuel prices, the price of LPG and the GST rates. I am willing to abide by their verdict. I hope the Hon'ble Finance Minister will also abide by the verdict of the aam aadmi.

Thank you.

August 7, 2022

What 13.5 Per Cent Reveals and Hides

The National Statistical Office's estimates of GDP for the first quarter (April–June) 2022–23 were released on August 31, 2022. The number that is prominent is the growth rate of 13.5 per cent. In terms of gross value addition (GVA), the number is 12.7 per cent. Given that the estimates of rating agencies, banks and the RBI ranged from 13 per cent to 16.2 per cent (RBI), any number falling within that range would, I suppose, be enough to gloat about!

However, there is a large world beyond statistics. This essay is about what the NSO numbers mean to millions of people who live in the real world and on who will be happy and who will be unhappy.

Numbers That Matter

I have constructed a table containing the corresponding figures for 2019–20 and 2021–22 and added the numbers for the first quarter of 2022–23. Since 2020–21 was the pandemic-hit year that witnessed prolonged lockdowns, I have not included that year's numbers in the table. I may point out that 2019–20 was a normal year. The year 2021–22 was touted as the recovery year; 2022–23 is the year in which one hoped there will be a full-fledged recovery. So the focus should be on the numbers for 2019–20, 2021–22 and 2022–23.

Gross value addition in Q1 (April–June) at constant prices (Rs crore)					
	Agriculture, forestry and fishing	Mining and quarrying	Construction	Trade, hotels, transport and communication	Financial, real estate and professional services
2019–20	448,703	82,696	259,728	662,305	796,851
2021–22	472,258	80,243	225,166	445,454	805,847
2022–23	493,325	85,423	262,918	559,723	880,313
2022–23 over (per cent)					
2019–20	9.9	3.3	1.2	–15.5	10.5
2021–22	4.5	6.5	16.8	25.7	9.2

Further, the numbers must be viewed from the point of the people who will be affected by the performance of the sector concerned. For example, 'Agriculture, forestry and fishing' affects the lives of the majority of families in the country. 'Mining and quarrying' and 'Construction' are important because the two sectors employ the largest number of workers who have low skills and little school education. 'Financial, real estate and professional services' is important because it employs the educated and skilled white-collar employees.

The benchmark year is 2019–20. A country that is growing must grow at a brisk rate over and above the previous year and the benchmark year.

It is evident from the GVA figures that while the economy did recover in 2021–22 over the abysmal performance in the pandemic year (2020–21), sectoral growth barely reached the level of output in the normal year, 2019–20 – except in agriculture.

Therein lies a poignant lesson: pandemic or no pandemic, farmers and farm labour have no choice but to toil in their fields to earn for their survival. They do not have the luxury of work-from-home! (The marginal increase in 'Financial, etc.' was statistically insignificant.)

Not Out of the Woods

Therefore, the growth that we must look for in 2022–23 is not the growth over 2021–22, but the growth over 2019–20. The last two rows of the table highlight the difference. While the growth in Q1 of 2022–23 is impressive when compared to Q1 of the previous year (2021–22), it is worrying when compared to Q1 of the benchmark year (2019–20). 'Agriculture, etc.' seems to have retained its spirit. The pick-up in 'Financial, Real Estate, etc.' is encouraging. But the other three sectors in the table tell the story of an economy that is not yet out of the woods.

I had not put 'Manufacturing' in the table because I did not want those numbers lost in a forest of numbers. The value additions in 'Manufacturing' in Q1 of the three relevant years were: Rs 565,526, 577,249 and 605,104 crore. In terms of growth, Q1 of 2022–23 recorded a growth of 7 per cent over 2019–20 and 4.8 per cent over 2021–22. My conclusion is that manufacturing growth is still sluggish because of inadequate new investment or low demand or both. Intuitively, I conclude that the MSME sector is still in the doldrums.

Slow Start

The crucial question is what are the implications for the future, especially for employment. The status of farmers and farm labour will remain the same and there will be little movement to non-farm jobs. Since 'Mining, etc.' and 'Construction' are only slightly better than in 2019–20, unless there is a strong revival, unemployment among unskilled and low-skilled workers will be high. The steps taken by the government to boost manufacturing are apparently insufficient and have failed to revive the

MSME sector. The opportunities for skilled, white-collar workers are growing but a major part of the Services sector ('Trade, Hotels, etc.') is yet to revive, thereby dampening job opportunities. (Note: the unemployment rate in August rose to 8.3 per cent.)

The RBI had estimated the quarter-wise growth in 2022–23 as 16.2, 6.2, 4.1 and 4.0 per cent. Note that it is a declining graph. We have started the first quarter with 13.5 per cent – lower than RBI's estimate. What does this slow start foretell about the remaining three quarters?

September 4, 2022

They Love Unemployment and Inflation

Last Sunday, the Congress party held a 'Halla Bol' rally against unemployment and inflation. It is believed that everyone is hurt by unemployment and inflation. It is believed that everyone is determined to reduce unemployment and inflation.

I am sorry that I have to puncture these widely held (wrong) beliefs. There are sections of the population and – hold your breath – parts of the government that are happy with raging unemployment and soaring inflation and will do everything that is possible, clandestinely, to keep the flags of unemployment and inflation flying high.

Let's begin with 'Who loves unemployment?'

Business and Government

Business loves unemployment. Because there are so many people chasing a small number of jobs, the bargaining power of the job providers is high. Consequently, wages are depressed. Wage increases are paltry. For example, agricultural wages increased by less than 3 per cent in 2021–22 despite the inflation rate being higher. The average monthly income of an agricultural family in India was Rs 10,213 in 2019 (source: Economic Survey 2021–22), hardly sufficient for four to five members for food, shelter, clothing, education, healthcare and leisure. Since the bargaining power of the employed – or even the self-employed – is weak, the average income of a family rises only marginally.

In a period of low growth or recession, the situation becomes worse for the average family.

Government recruitment bodies and public sector enterprises love unemployment. When there are thousands of applicants including graduates and post-graduates for a few hundred lower-grade vacancies, the appointing authorities acquire enormous power and discretion. Brokers flourish, money changes hands, scams occur. Because job-seekers exceed jobs, there is growing casualisation and informalisation of jobs in the private, public and government sectors. Labour welfare laws are thrown aside. The trade union movement is weakened considerably.

Crime syndicates love unemployment. There is a large catchment area for recruiting runners for drug trafficking, smuggling, illicit liquor trade, illegal betting and gambling, human trafficking and similar illegal activities.

Let's turn to 'Who loves inflation?'

Tax Collectors and Sellers

Revenue departments and tax collectors love inflation. Month after month, the tax collectors report a 'new high' in tax collection, for instance GST collection. They never report the inflation-adjusted number. In August 2022, the GST collection was Rs 1,43,612 crore (as against Rs 1,12,020 crore in August 2021), but adjusted for the average inflation in the last 12 months, the real value of the GST receipts was only Rs 1,33,559 crore. In the case of ad valorem taxes, even while keeping the tax rates constant, the tax collector can reap a bonanza.

Budget makers love inflation. The numbers in the Budget documents are in current prices. Allocations are in current prices. So, the Budget maker can claim that she has allotted more money in the present year than was allotted in the previous year. Few citizens will make the adjustment for inflation. For example, adjusted for inflation, the allocations in the 2022–23 Budget for Defence, Fertilisers, Food, Agriculture, Energy, Health, Rural Development and Urban Development were *lower* than the Revised Estimates for 2021–22.

Government debt managers love inflation. Since debt is borrowed and repaid in current prices, the inflation rate depresses the value of the debt. The borrower actually repays less than what he had borrowed. Apropos the above, note that the finance minister said that inflation was not her red-letter priority concern!

Sellers love inflation. MRP has increased significantly, notwithstanding that input costs may have increased only moderately. This is especially so in the case of essential goods. For example, milk prices were recently increased sharply across India both by government-run dairies and private dairies.

Exporters love inflation. For every dollar of the value of export, the exporter will earn more rupees. Of course, in the case of import-intensive exports, the windfall will be lower.

Lenders love inflation. It is an opportunity to raise the interest rates, even if the cost of money has not risen commensurately.

Business, especially large corporations, duopolies and oligopolies, love inflation. They acquire more pricing power, especially in the case of price-insensitive goods and services. For example, if you must fly from Delhi to Chennai tomorrow, you have no choice but to shell out up to Rs 50,000 depending on the class of travel. The facility of 'dynamic pricing' has enriched airlines, Uber and Ola, and the State-owned railways. If you doubt the assertion, please look at the 'profit & profit' statements of private companies for 2021–22 and the quarterly statements for the current year.

Contractors love inflation. Old estimates will be revised. Price overruns will be easily justified. Price bids of new contracts will be increased.

All Political Parties

Editorial writers love unemployment and inflation. If an editorial writer is too lazy to think of a new horse or donkey to flog, he can take an old editorial on unemployment or inflation and rearrange the paragraphs. No one will notice the sleight of hand because no one reads editorials.

And finally, ruling parties and Opposition parties love unemployment and inflation. In the hands of the Opposition, they are useful sticks to beat the rulers. The slogan will be 'Modi hai, to mehangai hai' and 'Modi hai, to berozgar hai'! The ruling party will turn around and say, 'my unemployment and inflation are better than yours'!

A day may come when everybody will love unemployment and inflation.

September 11, 2022

Whistling in the Dark

The Reserve Bank of India was disappointed when the GDP growth rate for Q1 of 2022–23 was below its forecast of 16.2 per cent and recorded 13.5 per cent. For the remaining three quarters, the RBI's estimates are 6.3, 4.6 and 4.6 per cent.

The estimated average of 7 per cent appears impressive but the truth lies not in the average but in the trend line: note that in quarter after quarter, the growth rate will decline. UNCTAD has a gloomy forecast of 5.7 per cent for 2022 and 4.7 per cent for 2023.

There are parallels. Since demonetisation in 2016, the annual growth rates in 2016–17, 2017–18, 2018–19, 2019–20 and 2020–21 were 8.26, 6.80, 6.53, 4.04 and –7.25.

Similarly, the quarterly growth rates since the fourth quarter of 2017–18 were 8.93, 7.56, 6.49, 6.33, 5.84 (2018–19); and 5.39, 4.61, 3.28, 3.01 (2019–20). Take a close look and you will find the declining trend over four fiscal years and eight quarters!

The RBI Tutorial

Sound economic policy is always contextual. While some elements of economic policy in a liberal, market economy will be constant, other elements must be tailored according to the circumstances. Mr Shaktikanta Das, the RBI Governor, has explained the context: 'In the last two years, the world has witnessed two major shocks – the

COVID-19 pandemic and the conflict in Ukraine. Now, we are in the midst of a third major shock, a storm, arising from aggressive monetary policy actions and even more aggressive communications from advanced economy central banks.' In an era when the United States is the world's largest economy and the US dollar is the reserve currency, the prudent course is to 'follow the leader'. The US Fed will not stop raising interest rates until America's inflation, currently 8.3 per cent, is tamed.

The RBI Bulletin for September 2022 has an essay on the 'State of the Economy'. The Introduction reads: 'We live in times of conflicting possibilities – elevated inflation and rising recession risks; economic stagnation and increasing debt; strengthening US dollar and weakening currencies in the rest of the world; easing supply chain pressures and reshoring; synchronization in policy actions and deglobalisation; balance sheet normalization and liquidity stress.'

The Daunting Challenges

The above assessment is true for all countries. It is only in India that whistling in the dark is regarded as an effective policy response to the challenges! In this essay, I wish to list the heads under which you may conclude whether the government's performance deserved a pass or a fail.

Inflation

The RBI's mandate requires it to keep inflation at 4 plus/minus 2 per cent. Retail price inflation has been above the 6 per cent limit for most of the past 24 months. Wholesale price inflation has been in double digits for nearly 12 months. The current inflation rates are: CPI 7 per cent, WPI 12.37 per cent. At the post-monetary policy press conference, Governor Das candidly admitted, 'We expect inflation to come close to the target over a two-year cycle, but there are so many uncertainties.' Because of differences between the finance minister and the RBI about the efficacy of monetary policy the course of inflation management is uncertain.

Current Account Deficit

According to the RBI's statistical tables, the current account deficit in Q1 amounted to USD 23.9 billion or 2.8 per cent of the estimated GDP, mainly due to the deficit in merchandise trade. Preliminary data indicate that the merchandise trade deficit had ballooned to USD 149.5 billion in the period April–September 2022 (source: MoCI). Gold imports were USD 20 billion. On the POL account, the deficit was USD 65.1 billion. After a promising start in Q1, goods exports in July, August and September have shown a declining trend: USD 36.27 billion, 33.00 billion and 32.62 billion. At this rate, the CAD for the whole year will exceed 3 per cent and perhaps be close to 3.4 per cent.

Rupee:Dollar Exchange Rate

At the beginning of the fiscal year, the rupee:dollar exchange rate was Rs 75.91. Today, the rate is Rs 82.32. On April 1, 2022, the total foreign exchange reserves were USD 606 billion. By September 30, the total reserves had fallen to USD 537 billion. The RBI has used USD 69 billion to ensure 'non-volatility' in the exchange rate market, yet the rupee has depreciated by nearly 8 per cent in six months.

Slowing growth, high inflation, worsening CAD and a falling rupee make the macroeconomic picture.

A History Lesson

The situation faced by the country is not without precedent. In 2012–13, thanks to the stimulus packages of FM Pranab Mukherjee, high gold imports and the 'taper tantrum' of US Fed Chairman Ben Bernanke, India faced the same triple challenges. When the United Progressive Alliance (UPA) demitted office, at the end of 2013–14 the CAD had been brought down to 1.7 per cent, CPI inflation had been contained at 9.4 per cent (which declined further to 5.9 per cent in 2014–15), foreign exchange reserves had increased by USD 15.5 billion and the exchange rate was Rs 58.4. That is a slice of history for those who want to read history.

October 9, 2022

Head Buried in the Sand

If you are invited to write an essay on the current economic situation in India, what would be your top two subjects? Most people would pick the people's top concerns: unemployment and inflation.

The Ministry of Finance (MoF) publishes a Monthly Economic Review. I did not think that a bunch of six young and enthusiastic economists, asked by the MoF to write such an essay for the Review, would consciously avoid the word unemployment as well as words such as malnutrition, hunger and poverty. (I wonder if it was whispered in their ears that the prime minister may read the article.) The group of economists knows but will not admit that the omission of unemployment, malnutrition, hunger and poverty is a grave dereliction of scholarly duty.

Why a Review?

The Monthly Economic Review is a valuable document. I expected that the 2022 September Review (released on October 22, 2022) would give an objective mid-year account of the current situation and the strengths and weaknesses of the economy; indicate the course that the economy is likely to take in the next 6–12 months; identify the headwinds that the economy may face; and capture the trends in the world economy, and their impact on the domestic economy.

The September Review is a slim document – 33 pages of text dotted with graphs and charts and 3 pages of data. The text is divided into six sections and signs off with a Conclusion and Outlook. The sections reveal the concerns of the government: 1) Fiscal Position, 2) Industry, 3) Services, 4) Credit Demand, 5) Inflation and 6) External Sector. The inference is that unemployment, malnutrition, hunger and poverty are not among the concerns of the government.

Self-congratulatory

The tone of the report is self-congratulatory. The last sentence sums up the tone and the approach: 'As is the case with batting in swinging conditions, balls well-left (policy errors avoided) will be as important as balls played well (policy decisions taken).' What the authors have omitted to mention are the dot balls (clueless against external threats) and the balls that almost got a wicket (rupee depreciation).

Every conclusion is intended to sweep the reader off her feet. According to the Review, revenues are buoyant, capital expenditure is rising, the quality of expenditure has improved and the *fiscal position* was healthy – until August. There is a grudging admission that government borrowing may lead to a surge in public debt. On *industry*, the Review cites several indices such as the PMI Manufacturing, the S&P GSCI Industrial Metals Index, the Business Assessment Index and the Index of Industrial Production and concludes that overall business sentiment has improved. On *services*, the Review is upbeat on inter-state trade, tourism, hotel industry, air passenger traffic, transportation and real estate and predicts that the sector is poised to emerge as a key growth driver.

Credit demand is growing at a healthy pace (16.4 per cent year-on-year) but tightening monetary policy and slowing economic growth may apply the brakes. On *inflation*, the Review has betrayed its evident bias. It absolves the government of any responsibility by throwing the blame on 'geopolitical developments'. On *external sector*, the Review is a mix of self-congratulation ('stabilized exports') and helplessness ('sustained imports'). It says that 'the widening of CAD should also cease' and sticks to the estimate of 3 per cent of GDP – a prediction that flies in the face of other estimates that CAD may expand up to 3.4 per cent.

Strong Headwinds

What has been said in the Review, though biased and self-congratulatory, may be forgiven because the document will be history in a few weeks. What is infuriating is the cynical and callous disregard of matters that concern millions of people. On the day he assumed the office of Prime Minister of UK, Mr Rishi Sunak warned of a 'profound economic crisis'. Even an imperious President of China, Mr Xi Jingping, characterised China's economy cautiously as 'resilient'.

The UNDP and the Oxford HDI have, in a report released on October 17, 2022, estimated that 228 million people in India were 'poor' in 2020 (which number worsened in the pandemic years). In the Global Hunger Index, India's rank is 107 out of 121 countries, a score that has declined in the last eight years. 16.3 per cent of all Indians are undernourished, meaning that they do not get enough food. 19.3 per cent of children are wasted, 35.5 per cent of children are stunted.

The unemployment rate is 8.02 per cent. Recently, 37 lakh candidates in Uttar Pradesh filled buses and trains to reach examination centres to compete for a few thousand Grade 'C' state government jobs, indicating the extent of unemployment among graduate youth in just one state. The only safety net for the poor (MGNREGS) could not provide a day's work to 40 per cent of households seeking employment in 2020–21. The Review does not pay even lip sympathy to the issues of unemployment, malnutrition, hunger and poverty. Nor does it acknowledge the strong headwinds of global slowdown, de-globalisation, protectionism, high interest rates, inflation and currency depreciation.

On October 22, the MoF warned on the economic situation and said that 'this is no time for celebrations and complacency' but the Review took a contrary view. I wonder what changed between the morning and evening of October 22?

October 30, 2022

Crucial Questions, Cautious Answers

In an unusual turn of events last week, the duration of the sessions of both Houses of Parliament was abruptly curtailed and both Houses were adjourned on December 23, 2022. It seemed that the government was keener than the Opposition to end the sessions early.

Before the Rajya Sabha was adjourned, there was – again unusually – a civil discussion on the Supplementary Demands for Grants for fiscal 2022–23 and the Appropriation Bill to authorise the expenditure of Rs 3,25,756 crore (additional cash outgo) and Rs 1,10,180 crore (where expenditure will be matched by savings). The very large amount included a small sum of Rs 500 crore for Defence capital expenditure for construction of strategic and border roads in the northern and eastern states of the country.

I opened the debate. I did not want it to be another fruitless debate where there are questions from the Opposition and no answers from the government. I flagged past experience and hoped it would be different this time.

It was indeed different. There were questions and, to my pleasant surprise, there were answers – some ambiguous, some cautious and some non-answers. The questions and answers, closely analysed, will bear out the apprehension expressed by former RBI Governor, Dr Raghuram Rajan, that growth in 2022–23 will be moderate and the economy will face heavy weather in 2023–24.

Now, to my questions and the Hon'ble Finance Minister's answers:

1. Since the Budget documents project a nominal growth rate of GDP of 11.1 per cent in 2022–23, what will be the inflation rate and what will be the real GDP growth rate? (It is a thumb rule that inflation rate + real growth rate = nominal growth rate).
   There was no direct answer. No break-up was given. To be fair, to my second question, the FM hinted that the nominal growth rate may be higher but gave no number or the break-up of that number. It was an unsatisfactory answer.
2. How will the government raise the additional sum of Rs 3,25,756 crore?
   (a) Government already has the money because it has collected more revenues than the Budget Estimates;
   (b) Government will borrow more;
   (c) Government expects the nominal growth rate to be more than 11.1 per cent and hence, even if it borrows more and spends more, it will meet the target of fiscal deficit of 6.4 per cent;
   (d) None of the above.

   The FM reaffirmed her resolve that the fiscal deficit target of 6.4 per cent will not be breached. She also hinted that tax collections, at this point of time, were higher than the Budget Estimates. Translated into simple English, the government hopes that buoyant revenues will yield the additional sum of Rs 3,25,756 crore. That hope and the implied higher nominal growth rate of GDP will put the government in a sweet spot. It was a cautious answer that leaves wiggle room in case growth is slower in the third and fourth quarters of 2022–23.
3. In 2013–14, corporate tax revenues amounted to 34 per cent of gross tax revenue (GTR). In 2022–23,

corporate tax revenues, as budgeted, will amount to only 26 per cent of GTR. Despite a bonanza of 8 per cent (roughly, Rs 2,50,000 crore), why is the private corporate sector not making investments?

The FM listed figures of investment (mostly promised, for example, under the production-linked incentive scheme rolled out for 14 sectors) but did not applaud the private corporate sector. Nor did the FM chide them as she did when she addressed the Apex Chambers. It was clear that she was in a wait-and-watch mood. Thanks to slowing demand, inflation, rising interest rates, unutilised capacity and global uncertainties, the private sector is in a wait-and-watch mode. With both waiting and watching, it will be a year of discontent on the investment front.

4. Among the four engines of growth, apart from government expenditure, which are the promising engines?

   The FM was cautious on private investment. She did not pick private consumption. She expressed a hope about exports, but we know that the trade deficit is soaring. It was a non-answer.

5. Real GDP doubled in 12 years between 1991–92 and 2003–04. It doubled again in 10 years by 2013–14. Will your government double the real GDP at the end of 10 years of your rule?

   The finance minister was stumped. She could not say yes, she was reluctant to say no. My assessment is that the government will fall far short of the target of Rs 200 lakh crore.

6. Since you want Rs 500 crore for Defence capital expenditure, will you please tell us if China has conceded anything on Hot Springs; if China has agreed to disengage in the Depsang Plains and the Demchok junction; if China has built and is building massive

> infrastructure like roads, bridges, communications, helipads and settlements and is amassing troops and weaponry along the LAC; does creating a buffer zone mean that Indian troops can no longer patrol in that area; and did PM Modi raise the issues with President Xi at Bali?

Since China is an unmentionable word, the FM joined the conspiracy of silence.

That, dear reader, is the state of the economy, the situation on the India–China border and the value added by a discussion in Parliament.

December 25, 2022

The Economy We Will Take into 2023

A new year dawns today but the long shadow of the past year has not lifted. The unexpected international financial crisis of 2008 determined the course of 2009.

The unprecedented pandemic of 2020 determined the course of 2021. So will the unusual concatenation of events of 2022 determine the course of 2023. The impact will be felt in all the economies of the world and India will not be an exception.

The Government of India, of course, disputes such a forecast. For the BJP government, India is exceptional. The government alone believes that in 2023 growth will be *higher*, inflation will *moderate*, the unemployment rate will *decline*, despite the US Fed continuing to raise interest rates net capital flows to India will increase and, notwithstanding the Russia–Ukraine war, global trade will rise. I suppose one could be equally optimistic and predict that despite the indifferent batting of India's top order, Ravichandran Ashwin will take India to a historic triumph in the ICC World Cup 2023. As the saying goes, 'if wishes were horses, beggars will ride'.

I wish government leaders and senior officials will read their own reports and the reports of world organisations. Here are some reports on the state of the Indian economy.

1. The Outlook: The balance of risks is increasingly tilted towards a darkening global outlook and emerging market economies (EMEs) appear to

be more vulnerable, even though incoming data suggest that global inflation may have peaked (RBI Bulletin, December 2022, State of the Economy).

2. On Inflation: Inflation may be slightly down, but it is certainly not out. If anything, it has broadened and become stubborn. India is poised to achieve the first milestone in its price stability objective – bringing headline inflation enduringly into the tolerance band during 2023–24. Yet, with inflation projected to turn up in the second quarter of next year, there can be no letting down of the guard. On domestic inflation: CPI core inflation continued to remain steady at 6.0 per cent for the third consecutive month. In terms of regional distribution, rural inflation at 6.09 per cent was higher than urban inflation (5.68 per cent) in November 2022 (ibid).
3. Global Growth: The Organisation for Economic Co-operation and Development (OECD) has pegged global growth for 2023 at 2.2 per cent which is 90 basis points below the forecast of 3.1 per cent for 2022. India's growth rate has been lowered from 6.6 per cent to 5.7 per cent (https://www.oecd.org/economic-outlook/ november-2022#gdp).
4. Global Trade: According to the WTO Goods Trade Barometer released on November 28, 2022, trade growth is likely to slow down in the closing months of 2022 and into 2023. The current reading of 96.2 is below both the baseline value for the index and the previous reading of 100.0, reflecting cooling demand for traded goods (https://www.wto.org > news22_e).
5. Trade Deficit: India's trade deficit during the 8 months of April-November 2022 was USD 198.4 billion as against USD 191.0 billion for the whole year of 2021–22. Of this, the trade deficit with China alone was approximately USD 73 billion (DGCI&S).

6. Current Account Deficit: The current account deficit is expected to widen this year. The International Monetary Fund (IMF) estimates the CAD as a per cent of GDP to widen to (–)3.5 per cent in 2022–23. The World Bank estimates a CAD at (–)3.2 per cent (Ministry of Finance, Monthly Economic Review, November 2022).
7. Fiscal Deficit: The Budget for 2022–23 promised an improvement in the fiscal deficit from 6.7 per cent in the previous year to 6.4 per cent. In December 2022, the government presented supplementary demands for Rs 3,25,756 crore. When asked what will be the source of financing, the finance minister hinted that the government will get the additional money through buoyant tax revenues and asserted that the FD limit of 6.4 per cent will not be breached. This was on December 21, 2022. Barely 48 hours later, the Cabinet met and decided that the subsidised foodgrain under the National Food Security Act (NFSA) will be distributed free of cost in 2023. The bill: Rs 2,00,000 crore which was not part of the supplementary demands (though there was a sum of Rs 60,111 crore tucked in for NFSA). My conclusion: 2023 will begin with the threat of overshooting the FD target (Ministry of Finance, RS Debates).
8. On Unemployment: As per the household survey of the Centre for Monitoring Indian Economy, the all-India unemployment rate on December 29, 2022 was 8.4 per cent. Of this, the urban unemployment rate was 10 per cent (CMIE).
9. On Recession: The 10-year US treasury yield fell by 44 basis points in November 2022 while the 2-year G-sec yield eased by 17 basis points, thus intensifying the magnitude of yield curve inversion and suggesting looming signs of recession (RBI Bulletin, December 2022, State of the Economy).

I am afraid the government is yet to realise that the things not under its control outweigh the things under its control. The Russia–Ukraine war, the disruption of supply chains, commodity prices especially the price of oil, and the new variants of coronavirus mean that India will step into a world of uncertainty in 2023.

January 1, 2023

Demonetisation: Three Dimensions

There can be no doubt that the Central government won the legal battle on demonetisation. By a 4:1 verdict, a Constitution Bench of the Hon'ble Supreme Court rejected all the contentions of the petitioners. Once the highest Court has declared the law, the conclusions of the Court are binding on all citizens. The dissenting judgement will only be an appeal to 'the brooding spirit of the law, to the intelligence of a future day'.

The Legal Dimension

What did the Court hold on the 6 questions framed by it?

1. The power of the central government under Section 26, sub-section (2) of the RBI Act can be exercised to demonetise all series of banknotes (of one or more denominations).
2. Section 26, sub-section (2) is valid and cannot be struck down as an instance of excessive delegation.
3. The decision-making process in the instant case was not flawed.
4. The impugned demonetisation satisfied the test of proportionality.
5. The period provided for exchange of notes was reasonable.

6. The RBI does not have the power to accept the demonetised notes (for exchange) beyond the stipulated period.

Leaving aside the technical legal questions, what will interest the reader are the answers listed at 1 and 3. On the power of the Central government to demonetise, the Court held that it was equal to the power of Parliament, provided there is a recommendation of the RBI to that effect. On the decision-making process, the Court held that the Central Board of the RBI had considered all relevant factors and all relevant factors were considered by the Cabinet too.

The Court made some observations that will interest the reader: on the question whether the objectives of demonetisation were achieved or not, the Court said that it did not have the expertise to go into the question. On the hardships faced by the people, the Court said that merely because some citizens have suffered hardships, that would not be a ground to hold the decision bad in law.

Thus, the legal issues were decided in favour of the government.

The Political Dimension

The answers to the legal questions may have brought those arguments to a close but a debate will begin on the other two dimensions. Editorials in the *Indian Express*, *The Hindu* and the *Times of India* noted them.

On two occasions in the past – 1946 and 1978 – high-denomination banknotes were demonetised through an Ordinance that was replaced by an Act of Parliament. It was in the exercise of *plenary legislative power*. The RBI Governor of the time refused to support demonetisation. Hence, Parliament passed an Act. The responsibility for the outcomes, good or bad, and for the hardships suffered by the people (they turned out to be minimal) lay with the parliamentarians who passed the law. There was a debate in Parliament and presumably all aspects were considered by the people's representatives before the decision was ratified.

Can the same be said of the demonetisation done on November 8, 2016 through the exercise of *delegated executive power*? Parliament had no role to play. Logically, the people's representatives cannot be blamed for the failure of the objectives or for the economic consequences. Cash in circulation has *increased* from Rs 17.2 lakh crore in 2016 to Rs 32 lakh crore in 2022. 'Black money' (or unaccounted cash) is *unearthed* so often by the Income-Tax Department or the investigative agencies that one has lost count. Fake currency notes are *detected* every day, including fake notes in the new Rs 500 and Rs 2,000 denominations. Terrorism – both terrorists killing innocent citizens and terrorists being killed – is *reported* practically every week. Financing of terrorism is *unabated* and the Government of India has offered to host a permanent secretariat for the ministerial conference on NMFT (No Money for Terror). Which of the objectives of demonetisation has been achieved? None. Parliament must debate these issues.

There is another question of paramount importance. Can the delegated *executive* power of the government be equal to the plenary *legislative* power of Parliament? In the case of the RBI Act, Section 26, sub-section (2), the question has been decided in favour of the government. But will the answer be the same if the question arose in respect of other Acts? Parliament must find an opportunity to debate this important question.

The Economic Dimension

The Court declined to go into the wisdom of demonetisation or whether the economic consequences and hardships were proportionate to the objects of demonetisation. The Court exercised restraint and deferred to the judgement of the government. However, as far as the people are concerned, what matters to them most are the *wisdom* of the decision and the *economic hardships* suffered by the middle class and the poor, the 30-crore daily wage earners, the MSMEs, and the farmers who found that the prices of agricultural produce had crashed. Moreover, after the third quarter of 2016–17 (when demonetisation took place), the annual GDP growth rate *declined* every year in 2017–18, 2018–19 and 2019–20. Then, the pandemic struck and added to the economic woes. The people will continue to debate these issues.

On the legal argument, the government won comprehensively. On the political argument, the debate is not over and Parliament must engage in it. On the economic argument, the government lost it long ago but will not admit it.

January 8, 2023

First Advance Warning of 2023–24

In 2016–17, the National Statistical Office introduced the wholesome practice of publishing the First Advance Estimates (FAEs) of National Income of the financial year that is drawing to a close. The estimates will be useful inputs in the making of the Budget for the next financial year. Although based on data available only for the first eight months of the financial year, and some numbers are extrapolated, the estimates contain valuable information. Revenue and expenditure data compiled by the Controller General of Accounts available up to November are also good indicators. They will help the finance minister arrive at the Revised Estimates for the current year and the Budget Estimates for the next year.

Estimates Are Mixed Bag

Estimates can go awry. Three or four months is a long time as far as the economy is concerned. No one could have anticipated the outbreak of coronavirus and its rapid spread by the end of March 2020. All the numbers in the Budget for 2020–21 went for a toss. A black swan event like the international financial crisis that hit the world in September 2008 put paid to the estimates of growth, inflation and employment in every country including India.

Some lessons and clues can be drawn from the NSO's press release dated January 6, 2023. Before I do that, I would like to recall the conclusions that I had drawn in the essay of January 1, 2023 ('The Economy We Will Take into 2023', *Indian Express*). I had set out the outlook for 2023–24 based upon information taken from official and reliable sources. I suggest we look at the FAEs and ask whether those conclusions need to be modified.

There are some bright spots: the nominal GDP (15.4 per cent) will be higher than the Budget Estimates (11.1 per cent). Revenues are buoyant and may bring the government more money. As a result, it will be easier to achieve the target fiscal deficit of 6.4 per cent.

Consumption-driven Growth

However, there are a number of dark spots too. Nothing in the FAE would lead to altering my conclusion (based on the RBI Bulletin) that 'the balance of risks is increasingly tilted toward a darkening global outlook and emerging market economies appear to be more vulnerable'. What seems to be driving growth in 2022–23 is private consumption (57.2 per cent of GDP). Going forward, private consumption will be hit by steady inflation and high unemployment. The other drivers of growth are flat – the much-touted government expenditure (10.3 per cent of GDP) will be lower than in the previous two years and exports (22.7 per cent of GDP) are flat amidst predictions of a slowdown in global trade (as per WTO).

The other concern is imports which will be 27.4 per cent of GDP. This represents a sharp jump from 19.1 per cent in 2020–21 and 23.9 per cent in 2021–22.

Higher imports without higher exports indicate that we are importing for consumption. This may put pressure on the exchange rate of the rupee, widen the CAD and trigger capital flight.

Going by economic activity, the two worrisome numbers are in respect of 'Mining and quarrying' (2.4 per cent growth over last year) and 'Manufacturing' (1.6 per cent). These rates are sharply lower than the growth rates recorded in 2021–22. 'Construction' will grow at 9.1 per cent in 2022–23, but this will be a decline from the 11.5 per cent recorded in 2021–22. A week after the FAEs were released, neither the finance minister nor the ministers concerned have explained the dismal performance of key sectors of the economy.

Production Down, Unemployment Up

The outlook on unemployment is also not bright. The biggest job-creating sectors are Agriculture, Mining and quarrying, Manufacturing, Construction, and Trade, Hotels, Transport, Communications, etc. Except the last named (13.7 per cent) there will be flat or tepid growth in the other sectors. These numbers vindicate the CMIE's estimate of unemployment (all-India unemployment rate was 8.3 per cent on January 13, 2023). Instead of addressing the underlying causes of growing unemployment (the message), government is traducing the messenger.

On the production side, the FAE numbers for 2022–23 are depressing. Conceding that the percentage change numbers of 2021–22 were over the pandemic-hit year of 2020–21, nevertheless, the percentage changes in 2022–23 in nearly all major heads point to a perceptible slowdown of the economy – for example, production of rice, crude oil and cement. Cargo handled at major seaports and airports will register lower growth rates than last year. The Railways will record lower growth rates in net tonne kilometres and passenger kilometres. The index of industrial production will be in low single digits in Mining (4.0 per cent), Manufacturing (5.0), Electricity (9.4) and Metallic Minerals (–6.5).

Persisting high inflation will add to the economic woes. The WPI of food articles will be 9.6 per cent, of manufactured products will be 7.6 per cent and of all commodities will be 12.3 per cent.

How will the finance minister address these weakness in the Budget for 2023–24? Sops or rhetoric will not lift the economy or alleviate the distress caused by inflation, unemployment and global recession. We need clear policies and determined action. Let's wait for February 1, 2023.

January 15, 2023

Budget (1): Text Ignores the Context

The Union Budget has become more than an annual statement of the estimated receipts and expenditure of the Central government for a financial year. It is now the principal vehicle to convey to the people the policies and programmes of the government. People look to the Budget for specific proposals as well as signals.

The voiceless, however, remain voiceless. They have no access to the decision-makers in the government and rely upon the political parties and the MPs to act as a bridge. A dominant government with a majority in the Lok Sabha is usually self-obsessed and does not consult the political parties or the MPs.

CEA Reveals Context

People and experts look to the Economic Survey that is presented on the eve of the Budget for an update on the economic situation. As usual, the ES for 2022–23 in Chapter 1 contains the 'outlook' for the next year. This year, the Chief Economic Adviser, after wandering without direction, summed up the crux of the 'outlook' for 2023–04 in two paragraphs that are reproduced below.

> 1.30. Even as India's outlook remains bright, global economic prospects for the next year have been weighed down by the combination of a unique set of challenges expected to impart a few downside risks.

> Multi-decadal high inflation numbers have compelled central banks across the globe to tighten financial conditions. The impact of monetary tightening is beginning to show in slowing economic activity, especially in Advanced Economies. Besides this, adverse spillovers from the prolonged strains in supply chains and heightened uncertainty due to geo-political conflict have further deteriorated the global outlook. Hence, global growth is forecasted to slow from 3.2 per cent in 2022 to 2.7 per cent in 2023 as per IMF's World Economic Outlook, October 2022. A slower growth in economic output coupled with increased uncertainty will dampen trade growth. This is seen in the lower forecast for growth in global trade by the World Trade Organization, from 3.5 per cent in 2022 to 1.0 per cent in 2023.
>
> 1.31. On the external front, risks to the current account balance stem from multiple sources. While commodity prices have retreated from record highs, they are still above pre-conflict levels. Strong domestic demand amidst high commodity prices will raise India's total import bill and contribute to unfavourable developments in the current account balance. These may be exacerbated by plateauing export growth on account of slackening global demand. Should the current account deficit widen further, the currency may come under depreciation pressure.

If the CEA thought he had done his job, he was wrong. He should have subjected the 'outlook' to rigorous analysis in the Indian context and laid out the options before the government to take pre-emptive or corrective measures. At the same time, the Hon'ble Finance Minister, after reading Chapter 1 of the ES, was obliged to share her assessment with Parliament and spell out the measures she would take. Both failed. As a result, the text of the Budget speech has no relevance to the context in which the Budget was presented. The 90-minute speech was a long whistle in the dark.

Three Doubtful Highlights

Three things stand out in the Budget: (1) Having failed to spend the money allocated to capital expenditure in 2022–23, the FM has bumped the Budget Estimates for capital expenditure in 2023–24 upwards by a whopping 33 per cent. (2) Having made cruel cuts in expenditure on social welfare programmes, the FM has sought to assure the poor and the disadvantaged that their welfare is paramount. (3) Having failed to motivate people to migrate to the New [no-exemption] Tax Regime (NTR) that she introduced in 2020, the FM has put out questionable calculations of how the NTR is a boon for the middle-class taxpayer.

None of the three highlighted points will stand close scrutiny. First, government capital expenditure. The FM has tacitly admitted that the other three engines of growth are sputtering. Exports are down; private investment, despite the FM scolding industrialists, is sluggish; and consumption is stagnant and may fall. The FM had no option but to enhance government capital expenditure. In 2022–23, against a BE of Rs 7,50,246 crore the RE will fall to Rs 7,28,274 crore exposing the entrenched weaknesses in execution of government projects. Ignoring the constraints and the absorptive capacity of the ministries (for example, Railways and roads), the FM has allocated Rs 10,00,961 crore! Even the votaries of capital expenditure are flummoxed.

Second, the promise to enhance expenditure on welfare. In 2022–23, under multiple heads – Agriculture, Education, Health, Social Welfare, Urban Development, umbrella schemes for development of SC, ST, Minorities and Vulnerable Groups, etc. – the government had short-changed the target groups, making budget allocations false promises. Subsidies on Fertilizer and Food for next year have been cut by Rs 1,40,000 crore against the RE of the current year. Allocation for MGNREGS has been cut by Rs 29,400 crore. What is left are only soothing words.

Cracking the Whodunnit

Finally, the mystery of the New Tax Regime. It is already unravelling. The subject requires a separate treatment. One thing is clear: government intends to abolish all exemptions from personal income tax.

Brace yourself for a rollercoaster ride in an uncertain year.

February 5, 2023

Budget (2): Misleading the Middle Class

In Budget 2023–24, the government sweetened the New Tax Regime and exhorted taxpayers to switch over from the Old Tax Regime (OTR). The Honourable Finance Minister said that her five announcements will 'primarily benefit our hard working middle class'.

The FM did not define the middle class. However, her government has defined the economically weaker sections (EWS) and notified that families earning a gross annual income below Rs 8,00,000 would fall under EWS. It was based on a report by the Ajay Bhushan Pandey Committee. We may assume that those falling under EWS are poor.

Who Is Middle Class?

Another study by PRICE (People Research on India's Consumer Economy) found that 31 per cent of households have an annual income of between Rs 5 lakh and Rs 30 lakh and they could be classified as the middle class. That's about 28 crore households. A household may have only agricultural income or it may consist of more than one income-earning person but not all may be income tax filers or payers. In 2017–18, the Income Tax Department disclosed that 1,47,54,245 persons returned an annual income of Rs 5–10 lakh and 45,08,722 persons returned an annual income of Rs 10–25 lakh. The total is about 2 crore persons. The number may have increased since.

For our purpose, we need to know how many income tax filers disclose an annual income of Rs 8 lakh to Rs 30 lakh. My rough estimate, based upon the various data points, is a maximum of 3–4 crore persons. The FM claims to have given relief to them under the sweetened NTR.

Cracking the Maths

Several newspapers have published tables (on February 2) containing calculations of tax liability for different levels of income under OTR and NTR and up to what level is the OTR more beneficial.

According to the *Indian Express*, the OTR is more beneficial – with less tax liability – up to an income level of Rs 15 lakh. (The table stops there.) *The Hindu* puts it at Rs 35 lakh. The *Economic Times* puts it at Rs 60 lakh. Other newspapers have carried similar tables. For senior citizens and super senior citizens, the OTR is markedly superior at these levels. The government has not contradicted any of these reports or tables.

I have before me an Excel sheet prepared by a chartered accountant in Ahmedabad. It shows the salary income, standard deduction, professional tax, deductions under Sections 80C and 80D, and deduction for interest paid (Rs 2 lakh a year) on a housing loan. At every level of income up to Rs 30 lakh, the OTR is more beneficial. If the assessee has business and other income, the OTR is more beneficial up to an income level of Rs 10 lakh and the tax liability becomes equal at levels of Rs 15 lakh to Rs 30 lakh. The consensus appears to be that the OTR is more beneficial for the middle class, as defined. The government's argument that the middle-class taxpayer will pay less tax under NTR is demonstrably wrong.

Goodbye Savings?

However, the more important issue is whether, from a taxpayer's point of view, is it prudent and beneficial if the taxpayer 'saves and spends' or 'only spends'. The importance of household savings in developing countries is universally acknowledged. There is little or nil social security provided by the government to the vast majority of Indians. Therefore, for 75 years, the government stressed the importance of household savings. Household savings and corporate savings are the core of private capital which can be tapped for investment. It is not natural for individuals to save; they have to be motivated to save. Hence, the government, through tax exemptions, encouraged individuals (and corporates) to save in specified instruments or assets.

The BJP government has turned the prevailing philosophy on its head. The government is implying that spending is good for the country's economy. I do not question the need for people to spend, but spending must be balanced with savings. 'Save and spend' is a far better advice than 'Spend as if there is no tomorrow'.

I have used the Ahmedabad CA's Excel sheet to calculate, illustratively, the savings, the tax paid and the disposable income at three levels:

(in Rs)	**OTR**	**NTR**	**OTR**	**NTR**	**OTR**	**NTR**
Income	10,00,000		20,00,000		30,00,000	
Savings	3,75,000	–	3,75,000	–	3,75,000	–
Tax and cess	28,100	54,600	2,95,651	2,96,400	6,07,651	6.08.400
Disposable income	5,44,500	8,95,400	12,76,949	16,53,600	19,64,949	23,41,600

Under OTR, the assessee will pay less tax and strike a balance between savings and disposable income. Under

NTR, the assessee will have a larger disposable income but no savings.

The government's intention – no longer concealed – is to move to a no-exemption regime. I believe in a 'low-tax, few exemptions' regime that will encourage savings and leave enough disposable income to spend. Besides, a strict no-exemption regime must have low taxes. Under Budget 2023–24, the marginal rate of tax under OTR is 42.7 per cent and under NTR it is 39 per cent. These rates expose the myth of a low-tax regime.

Thank goodness the government has left the choice to the taxpayer, but for how long?

February 12, 2023

Budget (3): Abandoning the Poor

Every FM will boast that his/her government has the poor at the centre of its policies and programmes. That is fair because there is a significant proportion of the population of India that is poor. Estimates may vary, but taking into account only a few indicators – per capita income, unemployment, food consumption, housing and sanitation – the proportion that can be classified as poor will be between 25 and 40 per cent in different states.

The pandemic years (2020–22), the persisting inflation (CPI inflation 6.52 per cent) and unemployment (urban 8.1 per cent, rural 7.6 per cent) have only made the situation worse. The start of 2023 has been ominous. Big companies are laying off employees in the thousands. High unemployment rates are creeping into the educated middle class too.

Who Are the Poor?

Growing inequality in India has exposed many truths. According to the Oxfam report, the wealthiest 5 per cent in India own more than 60 per cent of the country's total wealth while the bottom 50 per cent own just 3 per cent of the wealth. In their Inequality Report 2022, Chancel, Piketty and others estimated that the bottom 50 per cent got only 13 per cent of the national income. The top 5 to 10 per cent (7 to 14 crore people) flaunt their wealth, spend and consume, which gives the 'shine' to the market. (The annual production in India of Lamborghinis is sold out for 2023 and the company is accepting only orders for delivery in 2024. The lowest priced model in India costs Rs 3.15 crore, ex-showroom.) They are the ultra-rich. The bottom 50 per cent includes the poor.

According to CMIE, the total labour force in India is 43 crore. Of them, the proportion that is currently employed or looking for employment is 42.23 per cent, which is one of the lowest in the world. 7.8 per cent of all households (roughly 2.1 crore households) have no employed person. 30 per cent of employed (roughly 13 crore) are daily wage labour. The median monthly household consumption expenditure is Rs 11,000. These households are the poor.

The government's National Family Health Survey-5 revealed that of women in the age group 15–49, the majority (57 per cent) were anaemic. Only 11.3 per cent of children aged 6–23 months received an adequate diet. The proportions of children who were underweight (32.1 per cent), stunted (35.5), wasted (19,3) and severely wasted (7.7) were alarmingly high. These sections do not get enough food. They are the poor.

Budget Punishes Poor

Now, ask the authors of Budget 2023–24 what they have done for the poor, what they have done for the bottom 50 per cent of the population, what they have done for the unemployed and what they have done for those who do not get enough food. The answers are in the numbers in the Budget documents.

Under key heads that would have created jobs for the poor as well as brought them relief, the allocated funds were not spent during the course of 2022–23:

	2022–23 (Rs crore)	
	BE	RE
Agriculture and allied activities	83,521	76,279
PM Kisan	68,000	60,000
Social welfare	51,780	46,502
Education	1,04,278	99,881
Health	86,606	76,351
Umbrella scheme for		
Scheduled Castes	8,710	7,722
Scheduled Tribes	4,111	3,874
Minorities	1,810	530
Vulnerable groups	1,931	1,921

Allocations at the start of the year are irrelevant if what is spent by the end of the year is significantly less than what was allocated. The poor have been short-changed.

Going forward to 2023–24, there is no evidence of a change of approach.

	2022–23	2023–24
	RE	BE
	(Rs crore)	
MGNREGA	89,400	60,000
Subsidy on		
Fertiliser	2,35,220	1,75,100
Food	2,87,194	1,97,350
Petroleum	9,171	2,257
PM Swasthya Suraksha Yojana (Health Insurance Scheme)	8,270	3,365
National Social Assistance Programme (old age, disability pensions)	9,652	9,636
PM POSHAN (Midday meal scheme)	12,800	11,600
Atmanirbhar Bharat Rojgar Yojana	5,758	2,273

Hit in the Belly

It is only if the allocated amount is spent that jobs will be created or welfare benefits will accrue. Besides, any allocation which is seemingly more than the allocation in the previous year has to be adjusted for inflation and, in many cases, it will be found that the allocation is actually less. Every programme which directly benefits the poor has been given less money and, adjusted for inflation, it will be even less. Added to the above, there is no cut in GST (64 per cent of the total collections come from the bottom 50 per cent). There is no reduction in the tax on, or the price of, petrol, diesel and LPG. It is as if the FM is blissfully unaware of post-pandemic rise in poverty, inequality, unemployment, lay-offs, malnutrition, anaemia and child-stunting and child-wasting.

Is there any surprise that in the 90-minute speech, the FM mentioned the word 'poor' just twice? There is a Tamil proverb that describes the budget best: it hit the poor in the belly.

February 19, 2023

Pivot to the Bottom 50 Per Cent

The open, competitive, liberal economy created national champions. The champions were small to begin with but acquired the strength to be competitive nationally and, in some cases, internationally. The names that spring to mind immediately are Infosys, TCS, Reliance, HDFC, ICICI, L&T, Tata, Serum Institute of India, Biocon, Maruti, Bajaj, Hero, TVS and many others.

These national champions created wealth. They also gave birth to a large middle class made of employees and shareholders. Thanks to the large businesses, medium and small businesses flourished. The culture of risk taking was born. Indian industry shed export pessimism. Aditya Birla took an Indian manufacturing company abroad and pioneered a new trend of overseas investment.

India's GDP, in constant prices, was Rs 25.4 lakh crore in 1991–92. It doubled to Rs 50.8 lakh crore in 2003–04. It doubled again to over Rs 100 lakh crore in calendar year 2014. That is a lot of wealth. Per capita income, in current prices, that was Rs 6,835 in 1991–92, increased to Rs 1,71,498 in 2021–22.

We Failed the Poor

There was talk of India becoming a middle-income country although, in my view, that is some distance away. There is the boast that India is the fifth (no, a minister said, the fourth) 'largest' economy in the world, but remember India is not yet a middle-income country, not to speak of being a rich country. There is talk of India becoming a USD 5 trillion economy but, in my view, that is a meaningless goalpost. Even if the Indian economy crawled, it will reach that milestone some day. (A bicycle will also take the rider from Delhi to Agra, as will a Rolls-Royce.) These are, in economic terms, irrelevant. What are relevant and meaningful are the distribution of income and wealth, the sustainability of the growth model, and the impact on the environment.

By those measures, the Indian growth story has failed the bottom 50 per cent of the population. The bottom 50 per cent gets only 13 per cent of the national income (Chancell, Piketty, et al.) and holds just 3 per cent of the nation's wealth (Oxfam). There is, in practical terms, no wealth tax. There is no inheritance tax. Agricultural income is outside the tax net. Gifts to relatives are not taxable. Consequently, wealthy individuals find it easy to redistribute their wealth and income among close family members.

The bottom 50 per cent is poor because it has few assets, little income and no opportunity for advancement. There are millions of poor people but we pretend not to notice them. The spanking new bridge catches the eye, but the eye ignores the poor families who huddle under the bridge. There are children selling pencils or towels or pirated copies of books on the streets; they are poor. There are 30 crore daily wage labourers; they are poor. Every farmer who has no more land than the average holding of agricultural land (1 hectare) is poor. There is malnutrition and hunger among sections of the people who do not get adequate food; those people are poor. The poor and the lower middle class make up the bottom 50 per cent of the population.

New Core Constituency

The increase in the wealth of the country, under the prevailing policies, goes largely to the top 50 per cent. No political party has reset its policies to benefit the bottom 50 per cent. My pitch at the Raipur session of the All India Congress Committee that concluded on February 26, 2023, was to reiterate the party's commitment to an open, competitive and liberal economy (in order to create wealth) and for the Congress party to embrace the bottom 50 per cent of the population as its core constituency. It will be a decisive shift from relying on voting groups based on caste or religion.

There will be resistance. The top 50 per cent will resist because they will no longer be able to garner the bulk of the gains of a growing economy. There will be resistance from political donors who will hold back the modest amounts of money they give to the Congress party. There will be jostling for space with political parties whose core constituencies are based on caste or religion or narrow identities.

Boldly Embrace

Nevertheless, I would plead that the Congress party should boldly embrace the bottom 50 per cent of the population as its core constituency. There are many reasons to do so. First, it is the morally right thing to do. Second, it will unleash the energies of the bottom 50 per cent that underperforms in the present situation. Third, it will encourage more people to work or look for work and increase the number of employed persons (and the labour force participation rate). Fourth, it will foster more competition and efficiency. Fifth, the yardstick of 'bottom 50 per cent' will cut across religions, castes, languages, gender, regions and states. And, finally, it may turn out to be an antidote to the toxic polarisation of Hindutva (not to be confused with Hinduism).

The bottom 50 per cent of the population lives in conditions not very different from the conditions under colonial rule. It is not effectively represented in political parties or in the legislatures and Parliament. The bottom 50 per cent is waiting to be recognised and embraced, and it has the potential to pick a winner.

March 5, 2023

Putting Lipstick on the Numbers

On the Republican Party's campaign during the US presidential election in 2008, the Democratic Party's candidate, Mr Barack Obama, said, 'You can put lipstick on a pig, but it is still a pig.' That crushing putdown became instantly famous. According to Wikipedia, the phrase has been in use since at least the middle of the twentieth century.

I was reminded of the phrase when I heard the spin that government officers put on the NSO's estimates on India's national income released on February 28, 2023. Numbers do not lie, interpretations of the numbers lie – as we found in the weeks following the presentation of Budget 2023–24. In her Budget speech, the Hon'ble Finance Minister projected a GDP growth of 7 per cent in 2022–23. Since then, government officers, including the Chief Economic Adviser, have repeated that claim. It may well turn out to be correct, but behind the alluring number of 7 per cent lies the cold fact that, in successive quarters of 2022–23, the output has recorded a *declining* growth rate. According to the NSO's estimates, the growth rates in the first three quarters, year-on-year, are 13.2, 6.3 and 4.4 per cent.

Output Matters

In my view, neither the year-on-year quarterly estimate nor the sequential quarterly estimate of the growth rate reflects the true state of the economy. Ultimately, it is

	2022–23 (Rs crore)		
	Q1	Q2	Q3
Gross value addition *of which*	35,03,189	35,66,493	37,17,073
Mining and quarrying	82,664	65,594	78,732
Manufacturing	6,39,243	6,29,798	6,14,982
Electricity, gas, water	90,134	87,489	81,537
Financial, real estate, professional service	8,82,147	9,33,441	7,45,836
Gross domestic product *of which*	37,47,908	38,80,988	40,18,584
Government final consumption expenditure	4,11,243	3,32,450	3,47,661
Gross fixed capital formation	12,99,435	13,27,486	12,76,872
Exports	9,15,472	9,28,593	9,19,661
Imports	10,01,644	10,99,168	10,17,152

the 'output' of all our endeavours in each quarter that will matter. The NSO has measured the value of the quarterly output in terms of GVA and GDP. Please see table.

Remember, these values are *absolute* values, not rate of growth over the quarter a year ago or over the previous quarter. If the economy was growing at a brisk pace, there is no reason why the value of the *output* in a quarter should be less than the value of the *output* in the previous quarter or the preceding quarters. For example, if the manufacturing sector was in good health, employment was maintained and demand was robust, why should the value of the output of the manufacturing sector *decline* from Rs 6,39,243 crore in Q1 to Rs 6,29,798 in Q2 to Rs 6,14,982 in Q3?

Note also that the value of the output of Electricity, gas and water (activities closely associated with Manufacturing) has declined in successive quarters.

Numbers Don't Lie

If we look at the economy in terms of GDP, government final consumption expenditure has not been able to maintain its pace. Gross fixed capital formation has been up and down in the three quarters. Exports and imports are stagnant. There is hardly any indication of strong growth. Another set of worrying numbers is private final consumption expenditure. Ordinarily, consumption jumps from Q1 to Q2 to Q3 by about Rs 3,00,000 crore in each quarter. In 2022–23, the increase in private consumption has been barely Rs 1,21,959 in Q2 and Rs 1,68,005 crore in Q3, pointing to lukewarm demand. I believe that the fear of inflation, layoffs and retrenchment has constrained private consumption.

It is not difficult to estimate the GDP growth in Q4 which will end on March 31, 2023. If the best estimate of annual growth in 2022–23 is 7 per cent, the 'space'[2] that is available in the fourth quarter is only between 4.1 and 4.4 per cent.

Reality Check

The economy is facing strong headwinds: recession, inflation, tight monetary policies, protectionism and high fuel prices in advanced economies; the Russia–Ukraine war; sanctions that disrupt supply chains; domestic inflation; rising interest rates and EMIs; loss of jobs and unemployment; and political uncertainty. No amount of brave talk will hide these realities. The outlook for 2023–24 is not bright.

Nevertheless the chorus continues. It is disappointing that the RBI has joined the cheerleaders. According to the RBI's February 2023 Bulletin, the Indian economy will 'decouple from macroeconomic projections of current vintage and also from the rest of the world' – whatever that purple prose means. Further, according to the RBI, the Budget for 2023–24 is 'the instrument of decoupling and raising India's growth prospects'. This is from the RBI that finds itself unable to decouple from the US Federal Reserve System (the Fed) on monetary policy!

If you had read the previous three essays on the Budget, you will agree with me that the Establishment is putting lipstick on the numbers, but they are still depressing numbers.

March 12, 2023

The Rhetoric and the Reality

Once upon a time, the Reserve Bank of India was the 'go to' body for all matters economic. It was considered a cloistered institution, inaccessible to ordinary people, but independent and wise. Its reputation was unsullied despite many spectacular failures: the most notable failure was its inability to spot the financial scandal that stockbrokers and bank officials had brewed under its nose and robbed thousands of crores of rupees (1992). The recent failure was its connivance with the government, when the government embarked upon the reckless adventure of demonetisation (2016). The RBI has also been called wrong on many occasions in setting interest rates, but that is par for the course among central bankers!

Nevertheless, I believe that the RBI is a treasure house of knowledge. In particular, the Department of Economic Analysis and Policy and the Department of Statistical Analysis and Computer Services are the most reliable storehouses of data. Both departments have first-rate men and women who are capable of providing sound analysis and policy advice. The RBI's monthly Bulletin is widely read and relied upon by bankers, economists, scholars and policymakers. It would be a pity if the RBI allowed its well-deserved reputation to be dimmed by either intellectual laziness or external compulsions.

The RBI's Bulletin for the month of March 2023 has the regular essay on State of the Economy. It carries the usual caveat that 'views expressed in this article are those of the authors and do not represent the views of the Reserve Bank of India'. This is despite the fact that the authors belong to the Department of Economic Analysis and Policy and are led by Mr Michael Patra, currently Deputy Governor of RBI.

The Rhetoric

What concerned me was that the essay, which should have been a reasoned and sober assessment of the economy, has made rather extraordinary claims about the state of the economy. Here are some:

- The underlying strength of this expansion is evident in the persistence of elevated inflation.
- While the strength of the labour market has come as a surprise, it is actually reflecting compositional shifts: leisure, hospitality, retail and healthcare are hiring at levels completely offsetting the jobs shed by tech-heavy companies.
- India has emerged from the pandemic years stronger than initially thought … Year-on-year growth rates do not reflect this pick-up of pace because by construction they are saddled with statistical base effects.
- What if at least 50 per cent of the Rs 35,000 crore of tax relief proposed in the Union Budget is used by taxpayers for consumption and adds to private final consumption expenditure?
- What if even a third of the additional allocation of Rs 3.2 lakh crore budgeted for effective capital expenditure adds to gross fixed capital formation?
- Unlike the global economy, India would not slow down – it would maintain the pace of expansion achieved in 2022–23.

Brave words indeed. Let's examine the statements closely in the light of what we hear, see, read and experience. The contrary data are: *Inflation at an elevated level persists and has pushed down private consumption. *Jobs axed by tech companies are not the same as jobs available in the hospitality or retail industries. *Quarter upon quarter and even sequential quarters have recorded lower growth rates (Chart 12 of the essay). *The 'what if' arguments are totally speculative: what if the bulk of the Rs 35,000 crore is used to repay household debt? And what if the additional allocation cannot be spent by the states because of inability to fulfil the stringent conditions imposed by the Centre (as it happened in 2022–23)? *'India would not slow down' is a startling prophecy by central bankers, as if India has decoupled itself from the rest of the world.

The Reality

I meet and speak to a lot of people from different walks of life. In recent days, I have met writers, lawyers, a hairdresser, MLAs representing rural constituencies, a former mayor, a Tamil scholar, litterateurs, party workers, a medium enterprise owner, journalists, a headmaster, an NGO head, a hotelier and several young students. Not one of them expressed satisfaction with the economy. Their main concerns were inflation, unemployment, lay-offs, sluggish demand (especially exports) and subdued consumption.

Culling out the common points of distress, I have come to the conclusion that private consumption has slowed down and remains depressed. While government capital expenditure may have increased, government final consumption has decelerated. The hotelier runs a 21-room moderately priced hotel in an industrial town. His average occupancy is 9–10 rooms or less than 50 per cent. The SME owner supplies (against firm orders) semi-finished products to garment manufacturers and exporters. He has a 60-seat factory but he has to suspend production on some days a month.

He narrated the story of a very successful business group that manufactures and supplies garments to international brand owners: their factories that were running for seven days a week now run for five days a week. The industrial town has several hundred crores worth of stock and is offering discounts to foreign buyers. Germany has made it clear that no large export orders may be expected until next year. Both merchandise exports and imports have contracted. Borrowing costs are high and may go higher. New jobs are not being created in urban areas. The all-India unemployment rate is 7.4 per cent (CMIE).

What do you want to believe? The statistical and verbal spin of the RBI's monthly Bulletin or your eyes, ears and instincts?

April 9, 2023

Spin Doctors at Work

Of the top five bowlers of IPL 2023, four are spinners – Rashid Khan, Y. Chahal, Piyush Chawla and Varun Chakravarthy. To a layperson, that is surprising because one thought that T-20 was made for hard-hitting batters who loved to hit the spin bowler out of the ground.

Perhaps taking a leaf out of the IPL, spin doctors are in great demand in the current BJP government and the institutions under its governance. The latest crop is in the RBI and among the 'economists' bowling for the government. A made-in-heaven opportunity presented itself on May 19, 2023 when the RBI announced that it would 'withdraw' currency notes of Rs 2,000 denomination. The spin doctors argued that it was not 'demonetisation'. Recall that in 2016 also, the notifications and circulars used the word 'withdrawal' and not demonetisation.

Our minds raced back to November 8, 2016. On that day, the Honourable Prime Minister announced dramatically on national television that currency notes of Rs 500 and Rs 1,000 were no longer legal tender. In one stroke, 86 per cent of the currency in circulation was declared illegal. The consequence was CHAOS. No useful purpose will be served by recalling those horrendous days.

Defying Logic

On November 8, 2016, the government also quietly slipped in the decision to introduce the Rs 2,000 note. The spin doctors called the decision 'remonetisation'.

The people were learning a new word, demonetisation, and the other new word – 'remonetisation' – blew their minds. Why would government scrap the Rs 500 and Rs 1,000 notes and simultaneously introduce the Rs 2,000 note? Why could the old notes not be replaced by new notes of the same denomination but of a different colour and size and with new features? The Rs 2,000 notes made no sense when tested against the three declared objectives of demonetisation: to eliminate fake currency notes, to unearth black money, and to stop the funding of drug trafficking and terrorism through fake notes. The hoarders, drug traffickers and terrorists happily welcomed the Rs 2,000 notes because it made their jobs easier.

Despite the government, the people shunned the Rs 2,000 note. It was utterly useless as a 'medium of exchange'. Few shopkeepers and fewer service providers were willing to accept the Rs 2,000 note. Within a few weeks, the Rs 2,000 notes practically vanished from daily, routine transactions. Yet the RBI continued to print and issue the Rs 2,000 note until 2018. It has now transpired that the bulk of the Rs 2,000 notes continued to lie in the currency chests or vaults of the banks. The remainder lay, not in the hands of the millions of people who used cash, but in the hands of a fraction of the population. Why the Rs 2,000 note was introduced in the first place has elicited no logical answer so far.

Why Withdraw in 2023?

The logic-defying Rs 2,000 note also defies the next logical question: why was it withdrawn in 2023? According to the RBI's letter to the banks, the Rs 2,000 note was introduced to 'meet the immediate currency requirement of the economy' and had served its purpose! The ordinary people of India did not 'require' the practically useless

Rs 2,000 note. They met their requirements by using lower-denomination notes and the Rs 500 note that was reintroduced, inevitably, shortly after demonetisation.

There was no explanation why so many crores of Rs 2,000 notes were printed when the people had shunned such notes. The RBI's further justification was that the shelflife of the Rs 2,000 note was only 4–5 years. If that is so, the shelflives of the lower-denomination notes (Rs 10, 20, 50 and 100) must be shorter. Just as they are replaced with new notes from time to time, the Rs 2,000 notes could also be replaced periodically. More the spin to the story, the more the spin doctors are trapped in their own web of lies. And in the process, there is less faith in the integrity of the Indian currency.

Mr K.V. Subramanian, India's nominated Executive Director at the IMF, had the most amazing explanation: it was to lure the black money hoarders to keep their unaccounted money in Rs 2,000 notes and, seven years later, to swoop down upon them and unearth/seize their black money! That deserves the Ig Nobel Prize for the most bizarre story spun by the doctors. Mr Subramanian's true calling may be as an author of science fiction.

Red Carpet for Hoarders

Unfortunately, no sooner had Mr Subramanian presented his outlandish theory than the SBI announced that the Rs 2,000 notes could be exchanged by anyone without proof of identity, without filling out any form and without proof of the source! Many banks followed suit.

It is now absolutely certain that like 99.3 per cent of the Rs 500 and Rs 1,000 notes had been returned in 2016, *nearly every* Rs 2,000 note in 'circulation' will be returned to the RBI. The tribe of spin doctors will spin the story that after seven years of Herculean efforts, the almighty

Government of India has successfully unearthed all the black money in the country, put an end to corruption and vanquished the drug traffickers and terrorists and their financiers!

The spin doctors are smacking their lips and waiting for the next grand opportunity to prove that theirs is the best business in town.

May 28, 2023

Modest Man Predicts Modest Growth

In a refreshing departure from the norm of the Modi government, the Chief Economic Adviser has predicted that the Indian economy is on course to grow at about 6.5 per cent a year during the rest of the decade. Mr V. Anantha Nageswaran is a modest man. He was appointed as CEA on January 28, 2022 and has, mostly, maintained a low profile and spoken only occasionally. In recent weeks, he has been more forthcoming and I welcome that.

In an important statement at Kochi on Monday last, the CEA said:

> India will be able to achieve 6.5 per cent GDP growth in the remaining years of this decade, despite the headwinds and turbulence in the global economy ... The growth in the digital economy and investments would also enable the country to achieve an additional 0.5 to 1 per cent growth ...

Evidently, the government is no longer expecting 'double-digit growth' which was its pre-pandemic boast. Nor will the government emulate the golden period of growth between 2004 and 2010 (the 'boom years' according to the former CEA). The size of the GDP, in constant prices, at the end of 2022–23 has been estimated to be USD 3.75 trillion. If the economy grows at 6.5 per cent a year, the goal of reaching USD 5 trillion, already pushed back from 2023–24 to 2025–26, will be further pushed back to 2027–28.

Who Is Responsible?

A modest rate of growth is due to both domestic factors and the external environment. We cannot control the external factors, we can only cope with them. For example, the Russia–Ukraine war and the deliberate cuts in oil production made by oil-producing countries are beyond our control. If the war continued or oil prices rose, we will pay a price in terms of slower GDP growth. No one can or will blame the government for the adverse impact.

On the other hand, domestic factors that affect the rate of growth are the government's responsibility. A government must be fleet-footed and resilient to manage these factors. What we have seen in India is that the growth momentum was lost due to demonetisation in November 2016. The growth rate slowed down in 2017–18, 2018–19 and 2019–20. Then, there was a black swan event – COVID-19.

The economy was practically shut down. Prolonged lockdowns, a delayed roll-out of the free vaccination programme, insufficient fiscal support to micro, small and medium enterprises, and government's stubborn refusal to make cash transfers to the very poor exacerbated the situation. Thousands of industrial units were closed down and hundreds of thousands of jobs were lost forever. Millions started their long walk to their homes in distant states, hundreds died on the way. Nevertheless, the government persisted with supplyside measures and refused to look at the factors that affected demand.

	2021–22	2022–23
	(Rs crore)	
Private final consumption expenditure	87,03,540	93,58,695
Govt. final consumption expenditure	15,75,280	15,75,306
Gross fixed capital expenditure	48,78,774	54,34,692
As % of GDP	32.68	33.95

Unremarkable Recovery

As a result, the recovery after the pandemic has been weak and shallow. The numbers tell the story:

The total consumption expenditure, private and government, grew by just 6.3 per cent. While gross fixed capital expenditure increased by 1.3 per cent, the GDP growth rate for the whole year fell from 9.1 per cent (in 2021–22) to 7.2 per cent (in 2022–23). It is a fact that consumption, rather than capital expenditure, drives growth in India. Sluggish growth in consumption pointed to less money in the hands of the people or high prices or more pessimism about the future – or all of the above.

By economic activity (GVA), except 'Agriculture' and 'Financial and professional services', the growth rate of every sector in 2022–23 was less than the growth rate in 2021–22. 'Mining and quarrying' grew by 4.6 per cent in 2022–23 (as against 7.1 per cent in the previous year); 'Manufacturing' grew by a dismal 1.3 per cent as against 11.1 per cent; and 'Construction' grew by 10.0 per cent as against 14.8 per cent. All three are labour-intensive sectors.

While retail inflation has moderated to 4.3 per cent in April 2023, we are not out of the woods yet. Shaktikanta Das, Governor, RBI, has cautioned that 'as per our current assessment, the disinflation process is likely to be slow and protracted, with convergence to the inflation target of 4 per cent being achieved over the medium term'. He added that 'regulators cannot be oblivious to growth concerns given the outsized addition to the workforce every year'. CMIE reported that the all-India unemployment rate was 8.11 per cent in April 2023 even as the labour participation rate stood at 42 per cent.

The 6–5–8 syndrome

There was a time when policymakers in India had 'settled' for 5 per cent growth and 5 per cent inflation. That resulted in millions of people remaining poor and India rapidly falling behind China and other South-East Asian neighbours. I am afraid something of that kind is happening now. The present policymakers boast of Amrit Kaal, but no longer speak of 8–9 per cent growth. They seem satisfied with 6 per cent growth, 5 per cent inflation and 8 per cent unemployment. These numbers spell disaster for India. They mean massive poverty, rising unemployment and growing inequality. India will not become a middle-income country for many years.

We must reset our goals. We must aim at achieving 8–9 per cent growth quickly and aspire to double-digit growth. Those goals seem beyond the capacity of the present policymakers and rulers.

June 18, 2023

To Grow at 7.5 Per Cent or Not

The Reserve Bank of India's mandate is price stability. However, it has joined other central banks in adapting its mandate to the objective of sustainable growth. It is therefore helpful when the RBI lays out a path for the growth of the economy – a duty often lost sight of by the government of the day that is focused on political goals.

All the information that is available points to a period of slow growth in the world economy and in India. The essay in RBI's Bulletin (July 2023) on State of the Economy has, referring to the world economy, acknowledged that 'global growth momentum appears to be stalling, especially manufacturing and investment. International trade is also showing the knock-on effects of re-engineering of supply chains through muscular industrial and trade policies. Once again, the world's constituents are set on diverging paths …'

On the Indian economy, the Bulletin lists the progress and achievements: upgraded infrastructure, digitalisation, solar generating capacity, exports of services, favourable demographics, ebullient equity markets, etc. Some claims under each head are true. The Bulletin also notes the sequential moderation in economic activity, high unemployment rate, uptick in demand for work under MGNREGS, contraction in manufacturing exports, contraction in revenue expenditure, decline in net tax collections, increase in CPI (and food) inflation, hardening domestic bond and corporate bond yields, and unending fight against inflation.

Before and After 2014

There are always pluses and minuses. Despite the mixed picture, India's GDP (at constant prices) achieved an average growth rate per year of 8.5 per cent during the five-year period 2004–2009 and 7.5 per cent during the ten-year period 2004–2014. On the contrary, the average growth rate per year in the nine-year period 2014–2023 has been 5.7 per cent.

Why has the average growth rate slumped? Growth rates are boosted in the initial years of liberalisation and market-oriented policies. Steroids – stimulus packages – help boost the growth rate. The benefits of unconventional monetary policies, adopted in the United States and Europe to offset the global financial crisis and the pandemic, flow to developing nations like India. In normal times, however, it is the attention paid to structural deficiencies and measures to remove them that will ensure high economic growth.

Fundamental Weaknesses

In my view, the present government has neglected some fundamental weaknesses of the economy. Here are four:

Low Labour Participation Rate (LPR) and High Unemployment: The working age population (15 years and older) of India is estimated at about 61 per cent of the total population – that is 840 million. It will decline after 2036. The celebrated 'demographic dividend' has a short life. The bugbear is the LPR. In June 2023, it fell below 40 per cent (against China's LPR of 67 per cent). Female LPR is worse at 32.8 per cent. Why are 60 per cent of the working-age population (men and women) and 67.2 per cent of women not working or looking for employment? Now, apply the unemployment rate of 8.5 per cent to the LPR. (Unemployment rate of age 15 to 24 is 24 per cent.)

You will get an idea of the enormity of unutilised human resources. Increase in life expectancy and the spread of education are of no use if a full 60 per cent is not able or willing to work. The Indian economy is running on two of four wheels.

Quality of Education: The Annual Status of Education Report is a nationwide household survey that captures, among other things, the learning outcomes of children in rural India. ASER 2022 reached almost all rural districts. Here is a summary of the findings on learning levels in reading, arithmetic and English.

Standard	**Children who can read Std II text (%)**	**Basic arithmetic level (%)**	**Read English words (5)**
III	20.5	25.9	NA
V	42.8	25.6	24.5
VIII	69.6	44.7	46.7

There are also huge variations among states. The average years of schooling in India is 7–8 years. If these are the learning outcomes of our children in numeracy and literacy, how do we teach our children and skill them to take on jobs/responsibilities that require higher levels of learning and technology?

Low Productivity in Agriculture: According to the Economic Survey 2022–23, India's rice yield was 2,718–3,521 kg per hectare while wheat yield was 3,507 kg per hectare. China's yield per hectare (2022) was reportedly 6,500 kg of rice and 5,800 kg of wheat. That India has become an exporter of rice and wheat may have induced complacency. Going forward, climate change, migration to cities, urbanisation, water availability, and rising input costs will mean that, if farming must remain a worthwhile and profitable activity, productivity per hectare must increase.

Inflation and Interest Rates: Indian industry is competing to survive amidst high inflation, high interest rates (because of perceived high risk of lending) and high tariffs. All of them must be tackled vigorously and lowered.

The One-eyed Monarch

When did you hear the Hon'ble Prime Minister or the ministers concerned speak on these structural deficiencies? Never?

Do we want India's economy to grow at 7.5+ per cent so that we may become a middle-income country or do we want to trudge along at 5–6 per cent and boast that India is the fastest growing large economy in the world? The latter is the equivalent of being 'the one-eyed monarch of the blind'.

July 23, 2023

PART 3

Governance Failures

There were instances of misgovernance. I listed the collapse of the Morbi bridge in Gujarat; the policy confusion over the intrusion into India-held territory by Chinese troops and their continued presence on Indian soil; the lack of debate in Parliament; the Balasore train tragedy despite forewarning; the breakdown of the Constitution in Manipur and the racial strife that has cost hundreds of lives; and other instances. The government did not have the grace to admit any failure.

No Apologies, No Resignations

On March 31, 2016, an under-construction flyover on Vivekananda Road in Kolkata collapsed, killing twenty-seven people, mostly construction workers. Prime Minister Narendra Modi was appalled and shocked. He said, and these are his exact words translated into English:

> The bridge has fallen. This is not an act of God but an act of fraud. It is certainly an act of God to the extent that the people have come to know during the election about the kind of government you have been running. God has conveyed a message to the people that today this bridge has fallen and tomorrow she will finish off the whole state. God has sent this message to save this [state].

On October 26, 2022, a 143-year-old suspension bridge in Morbi, Gujarat, across the Machchu river, that had been closed for seven months for 'repair and renovation' was opened to the public. A suspension bridge in a town is rare; it is usually found in a mountainous area. It was always a tourist attraction and, when it was reopened on a day coinciding with the Diwali festival and the Gujarati New Year, it naturally attracted a large number of visitors. On Sunday, October 30, the bridge collapsed. The death toll was at least 135, including 53 children.

Truth under Debris

The only concern on Sunday–Monday was to rescue the survivors. Many were indeed rescued, mostly by the local people including about a hundred Muslim youth belonging to a neighbourhood called Makrani Vas. After Monday, there were no survivors, only bodies were retrieved. Questions were not asked on Sunday or Monday, and that was the right thing to do. But questions cannot be buried forever under the debris of the fallen bridge. As the 'facts' began to trickle in, questions – and more questions – are being raised. These are pertinent questions. Here is a sample of the questions (and the likely true answers in *italics*):

1. Was a tender floated to choose the contractor who will carry out the repairs and renovation? Most likely, *no*.
2. Who was responsible to appoint the contractor? Most likely, *the Morbi Municipal Council with the approval of the urban development department of the state government.*
3. Was there a structural engineering report on the state of the bridge and a blueprint to carry out the necessary repairs and renovation? Most likely, *no*. So far, neither the state government nor the Morbi Municipal Council nor the police has disclosed if there were any reports or plans.

Clock-maker to Contractor

4. Was the contractor qualified to carry out the work? Most likely, *no*. The contractor was a company called Oreva, a clock-maker (in Morbi town famous for its clocks) and almost certainly did not have the technical qualifications or previous experience to repair bridges. Oreva subcontracted the work to Dev Prakash Fabrication Ltd.
5. Were repairs and renovation actually carried out? Most likely, *no*. According to preliminary evidence presented by the investigating agency before the local

court, it appears that the rusted cables were only 'polished and painted' and not replaced; and the flooring was changed to heavier aluminium planks.

6. Did the contractor obtain the permission of the authorities to reopen the bridge to the public? *No.* The municipal authorities and the police deny any knowledge of the reopening or giving any permission. After the alleged 'repairs', no fitness certificate was sought or given.
7. What was the business arrangement? Most likely, *a sweetheart deal where Oreva would bear the cost of the repairs and renovation (not estimated) and collect fees from the visitors for fifteen years without any interference from the Municipal Council or the government.*

God and the Message

There could be interesting parallels between the Kolkata bridge collapse and the Morbi bridge collapse. In the Kolkata tragedy, sixteen persons were arrested on charges of culpable homicide and all of them were soon released on bail. Among them were persons representing the contractor and the subcontractors. A 3,500-page chargesheet was filed in parts and it was planned to add more pages. It was alleged that the engineering drawings had not been vetted by any independent authority. The chargesheet alleged that failed steel materials (that did not pass the impact value test) were knowingly used. The nuts, bolts and sand used were of poor quality. Sections of the media had insinuated that the accident was due to corruption. And there was a failure of supervision. After all these exertions, the trial has not started after six years! With a few minor changes, all of the above failures may apply to the Morbi tragedy.

After the incident, there were the usual arrests of minor functionaries (not the owners or the contractor or the subcontractor companies), the usual statements of shock and sympathy led by the prime minister, the usual visits to the hospital (which, overnight, got a new coat of paint to welcome the prime minister), the usual announcement of compensation, the usual promise of an independent and thorough enquiry, and the usual silence on resignation.

The word 'accountability' is absent in India's political system of governance. After the tragedy, no one apologised, no one offered to resign and, as the cynics would say, in all likelihood no one will be held accountable and punished. If God is listening – to borrow the words of Mr Modi – will God send a message to the people of Gujarat?

November 6, 2022

Playing Chinese Checkers

Some political observers believe that the Modi government will never be able to live down the humiliation heaped on the country by China's PLA forces intruding into Indian territory in March–April 2020. In an earlier essay ('The Dragon in the Room', *Indian Express*, July 31, 2022), I wrote:

> It must rankle Prime Minister Modi that he did not get the true measure of Mr Xi Jinping when both sat on a jhoola on October 11, 2019 at Mammallapuram in Tamil Nadu. Even while the jhoola was swinging gently to the cool sea breeze, China's PLA was in an advanced state of planning to intrude into Indian territory. On January 1, 2020, President Xi signed the order authorising military action. PLA forces crossed the LAC into Indian territory in March–April 2020.

At an all-party meeting called on June 19, 2020, the prime minister, in his concluding remarks, said, 'No outsider has intruded into Indian territory nor was an outsider inside Indian territory.' One would like to believe the Honourable Prime Minister's words but there is overwhelming evidence to the contrary.

Memory Loss

Mr Modi, of course, believes that the people of the country have forgotten those nerve-racking days. He is right. The people seem to have also forgotten other poor judgements and missteps – demonetisation, the no-warning lockdown, the largest internal migration of the poor (some estimates put the number at 30 million), the man-made oxygen shortage, the pyres on riverbanks, the bodies floating down the river, the Namaste Trump rally and, even the most recent disaster, the collapse of the Morbi river bridge.

Since March–April 2020, the situation on the 3,488-kilometre border shared by India and China has only become worse. The incident on December 9, 2022 in Yangtse in the Tawang Sector of Arunachal Pradesh underscores the bitter truth: China chooses the time and place of the intrusion into Indian territory and the government is clueless and without a policy. Thankfully, our forces are able to counter every intrusion, suffering, in the process, casualties. In Galwan in June 2020, twenty soldiers lost their lives. In Arunachal Pradesh in December 2022, government has admitted that seven soldiers were injured although there are other reports that suggest more soldiers were injured.

China Chooses Time, Place

The question is, what gives China the courage and confidence to intrude into Indian territory at the time and place of its choice? That is the question, among others, that Parliament wanted to discuss on December 13, 14 and 15, but both presiding officers rejected the request on the ground that the matter was 'sensitive'. It is a strange definition of parliamentary democracy that Parliament will be denied the opportunity to discuss a 'sensitive' matter. If Parliament can discuss only non-sensitive matters, I suppose the next debate in the Rajya Sabha, under Rule 267, will be on the finer points of the 2022 FIFA Football World Cup final match between Argentina and France that is due to be played. (According to Mr Derek O'Brien MP, in the last six years, every request for a discussion under Rule 267 has been turned down in the

Rajya Sabha.) The English word is desuetude – falling into disuse. Rule 267 may as well be scrapped.

Parliament can be denied but the people cannot be denied. The people must know that:

- After several rounds of talks, China has conceded nothing on Hot Springs.
- China has refused to discuss disengagement of troops in Depsang Plains and the Demchok junction. According to *The Hindu*, the Chinese military remains on India's side of the LAC in these two friction points.
- From eastern Ladakh to Arunachal Pradesh, China has strengthened its military presence and infrastructure (troops, weaponry, roads, bridges, communications, helipads and even settlements).
- The US Defense Department's press secretary disclosed that the US had seen China 'continue to amass forces and build military infrastructure along the LAC'.
- More buffer zones have been created. A buffer zone means that Indian troops can no longer patrol in that area (as they were doing before 2020). It can be expected that China will demand another buffer zone in Yangtse.
- Mr Modi met Mr Xi at the G20 summit in Bali in November 2022. The video clip showed that the two leaders, dressed in Indonesian silk shirts, shook hands. Mr Modi did the talking. Mr Xi did not smile or frown and, apparently, said nothing of significance.

Whither Decoupling?

Meanwhile, despite the hostility exhibited by China towards India, India is importing from China four times more than what India exports to China. In 2021–22, the trade deficit stood at USD 73.31 billion. One hundred and seventy-four Chinese companies have registered in India. Some 3,560 Indian companies have Chinese directors on their boards. The government's claim of 'decoupling' from China has been blown to pieces.

China is playing Chinese checkers, not an unskilled game like dice. In Chinese checkers, a player can move only forward or sideways. He can jump a peg but he must move forward. The ultimate goal is to move his pegs and fill the slots in the opposite (enemy's) triangle.

Since the government is in the dark about the game that is played by China, it is keen to keep Parliament and the people in the dark. That is why we don't know what Mr Modi told Mr Xi in Bali and there was no debate in Parliament.

December 18, 2022

Amrit Kaal Questions

We are in Amrit Kaal. We are supposed to believe that 'God's in his Heaven, All's right with the world'. Nevertheless, pardon me for being unpatriotic, I have a number of questions of the government. Ordinary people ask me these questions in the hope there will be answers.

1. Notwithstanding the undoubted development, does the government believe there is high incidence of poverty in India? What is the proportion of the population that is poor? If the bottom 50 per cent of the people own just 3 per cent of the wealth (Oxfam), will they not be considered poor? Does the government agree with the Global Multidimensional Poverty Index that estimated that 16 per cent of the population of India (22.4 crore) is poor? Whatever be the percentage, why does the government not talk about the poor? Why did the word 'poor' occur only *twice* in the 90-minute Budget speech on February 1, 2023?

Jobs and Food

2. Does the government believe there is massive unemployment in India? Is it correct that the 'labour force' in India is about 47.5 crore and the 'labour force participation rate' (i.e., people working or looking for work) is 48 per cent? Why is the rest of the labour force – nearly 25 crore – not working or not looking for work? Is it correct that between January 2020 and

October 2022, the number of people working was 45,00,000 fewer among men and 96,00,000 fewer among women? Does the government agree with CMIE's estimate that the unemployment rate is 7.5 per cent? Finally, why was the word 'unemployment' *not uttered* in the entire Budget speech?

3. What is the government's estimate of the prevalence of hunger in India? Is the government aware that in the Global Hunger Index 2022, India slipped from rank 101 to 107 out of 123 countries? Is the government aware of the widespread prevalence of anaemia among women (57 per cent) and child-stunting (36 per cent) and child-wasting (19 per cent) among children under age 5? Does the government agree that malnourishment – or the lack of adequate food – is the main cause of anaemia, stunting and wasting? Will the government explain the reason why the Budget allocation for the Pradhan Mantri Poshan Shakti Nirman (POSHAN) scheme or the midday meal scheme in 2023–24 was *reduced* by Rs 1,200 crore from the current year's? Will the government justify why the subsidy for food has been cut by a humongous sum of Rs 80,000 crore in 2023–24?
4. Will the government explain why the subsidy for fertilisers has been *cut* by Rs 60,000 crore in 2023–24? Will not the prices of fertilisers as well as the cost of production of food crops rise? As a consequence, will not the prices of food and food products increase? Will this not result in lower consumption of food by poor families?

Unfilled Vacancies

5. Is it true that there are *1,17,000 schools* in India that are single-teacher schools and nearly 16 per cent (16,630) of such schools are in Madhya Pradesh alone? Will the

government please explain how a single teacher can teach students in five classes in a primary school? Why are more teachers not appointed in these schools? Is it because there are no qualified teachers or no money to employ them? What is the 'learning' that the children acquire in these schools?

6. Is it correct that thousands of young men – and now women – aspire for a career in the Armed Forces or in the Central Armed Police Forces? Is the government aware that there are *84,405 vacancies* in the CAPFs? Why is there not continuous recruitment to the CAPFs so that when vacancies occur the selected candidates may be immediately appointed? Is the government aware that aspirants to these posts are the less educated and from the poorer families in the country? Is the government also aware that many of them will be from the socially backward and vulnerable sections of society?
7. Is it correct that in the 23 Indian Institutes of Technology (IITs) there are 3,253 *vacant teaching posts* out of 8,153 sanctioned posts? Is it also correct that in the 55 central universities, there are 6,180 *vacant teaching posts* out of 18,956 sanctioned posts? Since IITs and central universities are directly controlled by the Central government, why are more teachers not appointed in the IITs and central universities? Is it also correct that most of the vacancies are in the posts reserved for OBCs, SCs and STs? Are the posts vacant because there are no qualified teachers or no money to employ them?

Exiting Amrit Kaal

8. Is it correct that every year in the last nine years over 1,00,000 persons renounced their citizenship and left the country? And is it correct that in 2022,

> 2,25,000 persons *gave up citizenship* and left India? Has the government conducted an inquiry into why so many Indians – presumably with good educational qualifications – give up Indian citizenship every year?

It is believed that, in Amrit Kaal, 'the gates will open to greater happiness and pleasures of humans'. These questions, if answered, will open at least a window of opportunity to millions of people, not to great happiness or pleasures, but to mundane things like food and jobs. Will we get answers?

February 26, 2023

How to Diminish Parliamentary Democracy

The US-based Freedom House downgraded India to a 'partially free democracy'. V-Dem Institute of Sweden described India as an 'electoral autocracy'. In the Economist Intelligence Unit's Democracy Index, India has slipped to rank 53. In this decline, both Houses of Parliament and their members have played their part.

Readers can add their observations to my short list on how India's parliamentary democracy has been diminished. Here is my list:

1. Rule 267 of the Rules of Procedure of the Rajya Sabha (the Lok Sabha has a similar rule) is invoked by members of the Opposition to raise a discussion on a matter of urgent public importance. In the last several months, the rule has been invoked in both Houses numerous times in order to discuss matters of urgent public importance – ranging from the Chinese incursions into India to the report of Hindenburg Research LLC. The chair has rejected every motion. Conclusion: as far as India's Parliament is concerned, there is no matter of 'urgent public importance' that requires to be discussed setting aside the business of the day. You have to believe that the Indian people are so safe, secure and content that nothing that concerns them merits an urgent discussion in Parliament.

Presidential Prime Minister

2. The prime minister, if he is a member of the Lok Sabha, is the leader of the House. Prime Minister Modi is the leader of the 17th Lok Sabha. He is infrequently present in either House. He replies to the debate on the Motion of Thanks to the President's Address every year. Prime Minister Modi does not answer questions in Parliament; usually a minister speaks on his behalf. (I wish we had the Prime Minister's Question Hour like in the House of Commons every Wednesday.) Mr Modi's approach to Parliament is very different from the approach of, for example, Jawaharlal Nehru, Dr Manmohan Singh or A.B. Vajpayee. The prime minister has become 'presidential'. If prime ministers remain presidential and act presidential, not for long will India be a parliamentary democracy.
3. The House of Commons sits on 135 days a year. In 2021, the Lok Sabha held fifty-nine sittings and the Rajya Sabha fifty-eight sittings. In 2022, there were just fifty-six sittings each of the Lok Sabha and the Rajya Sabha. Many of the 'sittings' were washed out because of disruptions. Arun Jaitley famously said that 'obstructionism is a part of legitimate parliamentary tactics'. The whole winter session of 2010 was washed out on the demand for the resignation of a minister and the constitution of a Joint Parliamentary Committee. In that session, the Lok Sabha used 6 per cent of the allotted time and the Rajya Sabha used 2 per cent. Of late, the tactics have been refined. In the current Budget session (second part), the Treasury Benches have led the disruptions every day. Few sittings and more disruptions will render Parliament sessions irrelevant. Bills could be passed (as they have,

on occasion, in the past) without a debate. We can begin to contemplate a time when Parliament will 'sit' on a few days a year, debate nothing, and pass all bills amid the din and the disruption.

Parliament sans Debate

4. Both Houses of Parliament are forums of debate. Great debates have taken place in the Parliament of India. The China–India war of 1962 in which India suffered a humiliating defeat was debated. Allegations regarding LIC's investment in the shares of Haridas Mundhra's companies were debated. The allegations surrounding the import of the Bofors guns were debated multiple times. The demolition of the Babri Masjid was debated. Invariably, debates end without a vote. In a parliamentary democracy, the government need not fear a debate because it will always have, or is presumed to have, a majority of the members on its side. Yet, the current government refuses to allow debates. There is an old truism: 'The Opposition will have its say, the Government will have its way.' I am certain the government does not fear that it will lose its 'way'. What the government fears is that the Opposition will bring to light uncomfortable truths during its 'say'. Has India moved into an era of a Parliament sans debate? I fear so, and if my fear proves true we have to conclude that the ceremony to bid farewell to parliamentary democracy will begin soon.
5. Imagine that a session of Parliament is called. Imagine that all the members gather at the Great Hall. Imagine that all the members vote to elect a leader as the President of the Republic. There are no votes opposing the candidate. There are no abstentions. In fact, there

is no other candidate. The country celebrates the result as a victory of 'people's democracy'. Can this happen in India? It can, because we are steadily on a course to one-party rule. If 15 states are ruled by one party and if that party (and its steadfast allies) are able to elect 362 members of the Lok Sabha and 163 members of the Rajya Sabha, nothing will stop India from becoming another 'People's Republic'. Mercifully, that dreaded prospect is some distance away but it cannot be ruled out altogether. When India becomes a 'People's Republic', parliamentary democracy in India would have reached its final resting place.

March 19, 2023

Silence Is Spurious Golden

Karnataka is known throughout India – and the world – for many reasons. The most notable reason is the state's capital is Bengaluru, the acknowledged information technology (IT) capital of India. 'Bangalored' became a dreaded word in the US for flight of business and capital. The inflow of business and capital made Bengaluru a coveted workplace for young professionals, especially in IT. Karnataka's rank in per capita state domestic product (in current prices) is an impressive 4 among all states.

A Middling State

All these and more should have placed Karnataka among the top five states of the country. Unfortunately, it is not. Look at some Education and Health indicators 2019–21:

Education and Health indicators 2019–21

Indicator	**Rank**
Women who ever attended school	18 of 30
Women aged 20–24 married before age 18	19 of 30
Infant mortality rate	13 of 30
Stunted children	24 of 30
Wasted children	23 of 30
Underweight children	25 of 30
Households where any member has health insurance	20 of 30
Population that use improved sanitation facility	17 of 30
Overall HDI	14 of 30

* On many indicators, Karnataka has *worsened* from its rank in 2015–16.

That is not the end of Karnataka's woes. After the 15th general election to the Karnataka Assembly in 2018, there have been four short-lived governments whose lifespans were 6 days, 1 year 64 days, 2 years 2 days, and the current one since July 28, 2021 (whose term will end after the next election on May 10, 2023). The villain of this sordid nataka (drama) of instability is, without dispute, the BJP.

No Reasoned Debate

The consequences of unstable and short-lived governments were predictable.

In the people's perception, the current government is the most corrupt government in the state's history and is deservedly called the '40 per cent sarkara (government)'.

That phrase was taken from the Karnataka Contractors' Association's official letter accusing the government of demanding and accepting 40 per cent commission or bribe for every decision of the government. Moreover, there is a long list of broken promises of the BJP spanning agriculture, education, healthcare, employment, infrastructure and the economy. Besides, the social and political discourse in the last four years has centred on useless controversies like hijab, halal, love jihad, the Anti-Conversion Bill and even Tipu Sultan, who ruled between 1782 and 1799!

One would have expected that the debate during the ongoing election campaign would revolve around the real issues that concern the people and which are thrown up in every survey or opinion poll – unemployment, inflation, infrastructure and corruption. Some 2,58,000 government posts are vacant. Since 2020, 1,258 companies have shut down. Thirteen PSUs are non-functional. There are multiple allegations of scams.

Polarising Agenda

Sadly, the debate has been surreal. When a reference was made to an allegedly corrupt chief minister, it was portrayed as a charge that the entire Lingayat community to which the chief minister belongs was corrupt. The Union home minister warned the voters that if the Congress was elected to power 'there will be riots in Karnataka'. Leading lights of the BJP (which has not fielded any Muslim candidate in the 224 constituencies) openly declared 'we do not want the votes of Muslims'. A statement in the Congress's manifesto to the effect that decisive action would be taken under law against hate-mongering by organisations like Bajrang Dal and Popular Front of India, including a ban, was distorted to mean that worshippers of Lord Hanuman (Bajrang Balis) would be thrown into jail: the prime minister magically transformed Bajrang Dal (a right-wing organisation) into Bajrang Balis (devotees of Lord Hanuman)!

More shocking was the appeal of the Union home minister to the people of Karnataka to 'hand over the state to Mr Modi'. Notwithstanding a federal system, will the prime minister rule every state, municipality and panchayat? The BJP's manifesto promised to push the idea of a Uniform Civil Code and the National Register of Citizens. Both issues have divided and polarised many states in northern and north-eastern India.

The Congress party, in its manifesto, gave 'five guarantees' that would cost, additionally, Rs 30,000 to 35,000 crore a year. Not to be outdone, the BJP's manifesto promised three subsidised gas cylinders a year to coincide with three Hindu festivals; one-half litre of milk daily to every BPL family; and a subsidised canteen scheme serving a meal (pictured) consisting of a bowl of rice, dal, sambar, curd and six cups of vegetables! Meanwhile, the prime minister warned against the 'freebie' culture!

The top two leaders of the ruling party – the prime minister and the home minister – made no attempt to defend the record of the state government. They were silent on the real issues that concerned the people; the silence was certainly not golden. Their speeches became shriller by the day and the campaign was entirely about the 'abuses' suffered by the prime minister; about Lord Shiva; about Lord Hanuman; about Bajrang Balis. The scene looked like a battleground from the pages of history going back to the era of the Mahabharata where an entrenched ruling class was challenged by the former rulers. Will history repeat itself?

May 7, 2023

Balasore Train Accident: Man-made Disaster

Since Friday, June 2, 2023, the most discussed issue in the country is the accident at Balasore involving three trains (two moving passenger trains and one stationary goods train). All facts concerning the accident point to one conclusion: it was a man-made disaster that was waiting to happen.

A suspicion has been sowed by the government that there were mischief-makers behind the tragedy. Maybe. If there were mischief, it was not the only one. Mischief means harm, damage, injury. There is a long list of acts of omission and commission in the last nine years that contributed to the accident that has cost 275 lives and wrecked the lives of hundreds of families.

Misplaced Priorities

1. On average, the Indian Railways (IR) carries 2.2 crore passengers a day, mostly people belonging to the poor and middle classes. Their travel is subsidised. However, except the subsidy, the IR is biased in favour of the rich. The result: priority for new trains over track maintenance and renewal; Vande Bharat and Tejas trains over capital expenditure on signalling and telecommunication; vanity projects (bullet train) over filling of the humongous number of vacancies in sanctioned posts; and speed over safety.

2. Of the total capital expenditure of Rs 1,39,245 crore in 2020–21, the amount spent on 'track renewal' was *8.6 per cent* and on 'signalling and telecommunication' *1.4 per cent*, showing the low priority to matters that are crucial for safety. The percentages are estimated to be 7.2 per cent and 1.7 per cent in the Budget of 2023–24.
3. The IR has a depreciation reserve fund for replacement and renewal of overaged assets. The fund had a meagre balance of *Rs 585 crore* on March 31, 2021. The CAG observed 'the amount is insignificant compared to the actual amount required'. Consequently, the value of assets to be replaced (called the 'throw forward') had soared to *Rs 94,873 crore* by the end of 2020–21, of which *Rs 58,459 crore* was on account of track renewal. The backlog in signalling and telecommunication works was *Rs 1,801 crore* (CAG's Report No. 23, December 2022).
4. In April 2001, a Railway Safety Fund was created. Its scope was enlarged to include safety works. The source of funds was through transfer of the cess on diesel. At the end of 2020–21, the fund had a balance of only *Rs 512 crore.* Typical of the Modi government, another fund called Rashtriya Rail Sanraksha Kosh was created in 2017–18 and was promised Rs 20,000 per year for 5 years. However, it received only Rs 20,000 crore in the 4 years between 2017 and 2021!

Forewarned

5. The CAG submitted another report for the year ended March 2021 on December 21, 2022 (Report No. 22). It was, prophetically, on 'Derailment in Indian Railways'. After the introduction, the CAG observed, 'Proper maintenance of the railway track is a prerequisite for

the train operation without accidents.' Track recording cars (TRCs) are used for inspection. The shortfall in TRC inspections ranged from 30 per cent in one zonal railway to 100 per cent in four zonal railways. The CAG concluded that 'the non-deployment of TRCs led to non-checking of track parameters having implications on overall safety of train operations including derailments'. The main causes were poor planning, idle track machines, vacancies in the workforce and lack of training of permanent way staff.

6. In the signal and telecommunication department, the major constraint was 'system/technological deficiencies'. Most serious accidents occurred due to collisions and signal passing at danger (SPAD). SPAD was caused by violation of rules, working beyond stipulated duty hours, defective vigilance control devices and absence of route learning of loco crew.
7. On February 9, 2023, the Principal Chief Operations Manager of South Western Railway wrote a letter revealing a serious incident that had occurred on the previous day. He identified a serious flaw where the route of despatch got altered after a train had started on signals with correct route showing in the stationmaster's panel – a serious violation of the basic principles of interlocking. He urged immediate steps to rectify the flaws in the signalling system. *The Print*, which reviewed the letter, reported that there was a dearth of gangmen, that stationmasters worked beyond 12 hours, and that 3,11,000 posts out of 14,75,623 Group C posts and 3,018 out of 18,881 gazetted cadre posts were vacant.

Gross Negligence

8. In 2011–12, IR had developed a train collision avoidance system (TCAS). In 2022, the Modi

government renamed it Kavach but there was little progress. IR has a total route length of 68,043 kilometres but the system has been installed in just 1,445 kilometres (*2 per cent*).

9. Railway finances are in a total mess. The merger of the Railway Budget with the General Budget has increased its opaqueness and sheltered it from scrutiny. A separate commission of inquiry must examine IR finances and recommend a path to recovery.

Mr Ashwini Vaishnaw joined the government on July 7, 2021. He is the Minister of Electronics and Information Technology (which he obviously enjoys); the Minister of Communications (which he may have forgotten); and the Minister of Railways (where, it is claimed, he has been 'on the job' since June 3, 2023) – better late than never.

That India cannot afford or find a full-time minister to hold the Railway portfolio tells you the sad story of the Indian Railways.

June 11, 2023

Incompetence, Injury and Insult

Article 355 of the Constitution reads as under:

> It shall be the duty of the Union to protect every State against external aggression and internal disturbance and to ensure that the government of every State is carried on in accordance with the provisions of this Constitution.

The Article is significant in more ways than one. The Union (Central government) has the duty to protect every state, not to undermine or destroy it. Thus Article 355 is an affirmation of the federal nature of the Indian State.

The Central government is also obliged to ensure that every state is governed according to the Constitution. It is a reminder to the Central government that it cannot be a bystander when a state is misgoverned or not governed at all. These are two distinct obligations.

The Union is a constitutional concept. Ultimately, it is men and women who act and speak on behalf of the Union government. That body of men and women is the council of ministers. The lynchpin of the council of ministers is the prime minister.

Twin Obligations

In the case of Manipur, both obligations are being violated every day since May 3, 2023. Instead of discharging the duties imposed by Article 355, the Union (that is, the council of ministers and the prime minister) is violating the Constitution. Since May 3, the prime minister has not uttered a word on Manipur – not even appeal for peace. Nor has he considered it necessary to visit Manipur. Meanwhile, over 120 people have been killed.

If some critics think this to be madness, we must examine the reasons behind the madness. I can think of the following reasons:

1. Manipur is ruled by the BJP and if the Central government reprimanded or dismissed the state government it may be a self-inflicted wound. So much for the boast of '*my country above my party*'.
2. Mr Narendra Modi may wish to dissociate himself from the unpopular Mr Biren Singh, chief minister of Manipur. So much for the boast of '*double-engine government*'.
3. Manipur is distant. What happens in Manipur has no reverberations in the rest of the country. So much for the boast of '*Act East*'.
4. Let the Meiteis and the Kukis fight. With the support of the Meitei-controlled state government and the Meitei-dominated BJP, the Meiteis will ultimately prevail. So much for the boast of '*sabka saath, sabka vikas, sabka vishwas*'.

If one or more of the above reasons is true, it is evident that the Manipur policy of the Central government is a cynical mixture of selfishness and callousness.

Black Day Repeated

May 3 is a black day in the history of Manipur. Thirty years ago, on May 3, 1993, there were violent clashes between Meitei Hindus and Meitei Muslims (Pangals) and over a hundred people were killed. History repeated itself on May 3, 2023. This time, the violent conflict is between Meiteis and Kukis. The trigger was an ill-advised order of the High Court of Manipur.

The Meitei community has demanded for long that Meiteis should be included in the list of Scheduled Tribes for Manipur. Successive state governments, advisedly, did not act upon it because there were conflicting interests in a state that is comprised of, mostly, three communities – Meiteis, Kukis and Nagas. The governments were accused of 'dragging their feet', but there was a larger purpose in not taking a quick decision. Before Independence, the Meiteis were listed as one of the tribes of Manipur but the community was not included in the Constitution (Scheduled Tribes) Order, 1950. Presently, most Meiteis are categorised in the general category; about 17 per cent are OBCs.

The political balance among the three major communities is delicate. Of the sixty constituencies in the legislative assembly, forty are dominated by Meiteis, ten by the Kukis and ten by the Nagas. The Kukis and the Nagas are among thirty-six communities categorised as Scheduled Tribes. If Meiteis are categorised as ST, it may make little difference to the electoral map but there are implications for owning land in notified tribal areas and government jobs.

Ill-advised Direction

As I noted, the trigger was the judgement of Mr Justice Muralidaran, acting chief justice of Manipur. Noting that the state government had not submitted a recommendation on inclusion of Meiteis in the ST list for ten years, the court directed the state government to send a recommendation to the Central government in *four weeks*. There is much that can be said on both sides, but it was certainly not an issue on which the court should have issued a direction.

The court ought to have lobbed the ball into the corner of the political institutions such as the legislative assembly and the Commission for the Scheduled Tribes.

A thirty-member delegation of BJP MLAs was not given an appointment by the prime minister. Ten Opposition parties led by a former chief minister of Manipur, Mr Ibobi Singh, waited in vain for an appointment. The Honourable Prime Minister left the state of Manipur to burn. Incompetence, neglect and partisanship have marked the tenure of the Biren Singh government in Manipur. Insult has been added now.

One engine in Manipur (state government) has run out of fuel; the other engine (Central government) has decided to decouple itself and hide in the loco shed. Thanks to the double engine, Manipur is a boiling cauldron. Cry, my beloved country.

June 25, 2023

Manipur Burns, Government Fiddles

I hold the view that if normal people of average intelligence behave as if they have lost their senses, it is because there is a method in their madness. Nothing illustrates this better than the conduct of the Government of India while the state of Manipur burns.

The BJP holds the reins of government in Delhi and in Imphal, the capital of Manipur. There are channels of communication within the party. There are administrative channels of communication from the Governor and the Intelligence Bureau to civil society organisations and the media.

Ethnic Cleansing?

What is happening in Manipur is not the occasional brawl; it is not opportunistic crime; it is not random incidents of murder or rape; it is not plunder and loot for gain. It is – let us not mince words – the beginning of ethnic cleansing.

The dreaded phrase has come to haunt India. 'Ethnic cleansing' has been defined as the attempt to get rid (through deportation, displacement or even mass killing) members of an unwanted ethnic group in order to establish an ethnically homogeneous geographic area (history.com editors). Historians cite examples of the massacre of Armenians during World War I and the Holocaust in which six million European Jews were killed. Serbia in

Europe and some African countries have witnessed ethnic cleansing.

Manipur was recognised by the Constitution as a state with a defined territory in which three major ethnic groups live. By and large, the Meitei live in the valley (forty seats in the state assembly), the Kuki-Zomi live in four districts (ten seats) and the Naga live in the four hill districts (ten seats). Irrespective of the political party, the MLA identifies with his/her tribe. Effectively, Meitei rule the state.

Today, from all reports that I have received or read, there is practically no Kuki-Zomi in the valley and there is no Meitei in the areas dominated by the Kuki-Zomi. That includes, I am told, government employees. Mr Babu Verghese, a journalist who visited Manipur, told Mr Karan Thapar that 'there are no Meitei in the hills and no Kuki in the valley and, therefore, there is effective demographic and geographical separation'. Violence has forced hundreds of families to migrate to safer districts/places. I am also told that the chief minister and his ministers work out of their home offices and do not – or cannot – travel to the affected areas. It is obvious that their writ does not run beyond the neighbourhood of their homes and offices. None of the ethnic groups trusts the Manipur police. The Central Armed Police Forces were under some kind of restraint until recently. The Army has been given a limited mandate. As a result, killing continues for several weeks after May 3. No one believes the official numbers of the casualties. Women are the worst sufferers. Rape and gang rape are weapons that are employed to humiliate and terrorise the vulnerable people in a conflict area. Hundreds have suffered such violence and humiliation. One of them was the wife of a Kargil hero.

The greater danger is that once ethnic cleansing begins, it is contagious. Meitei living in neighbouring Mizoram have been warned to leave the state. Six hundred Meitei may have left.

Ignorance or Inaction?

The case of the alleged molestation of two women on May 4 illustrates the dire situation of Manipur. One of the women charged that the police stood and watched while the mob took away the women. The victims were able to lodge an FIR only on May 18. Another FIR was lodged on June 21. The woman told the police that she had recognised some members of the mob including 'a friend of her brother's'. No action was taken for seventy-five days. The SP, DGP and the chief secretary (CS) did nothing. On receiving a letter from an American Manipur Association about the incident of May 4, the National Commission for Women 'informed' the CS and the DGP on June 19, but did nothing more. The National Human Rights Commission took no notice. Despite the many channels of communication, the chief minister claimed that he had no knowledge of the incident! All were jolted out of their slumber only when a video of the horrific crime went viral on or about July 19. If this is not a case of the complete collapse of constitutional government in Manipur, we might as well repeal Articles 355 and 356 of the Constitution.

The Nellie (Assam) massacre of 1983 was discussed in Parliament. Yet, since July 20, the Treasury Benches and the Opposition in Parliament cannot agree on the rule under which a debate on the Manipur crisis should be held. The government stubbornly maintains that the Honourable Prime Minister will not make a statement in Parliament. The impasse points to the depressing conclusion that Parliament has become dysfunctional and has failed the people of the country.

A Heap of Ruins

A dysfunctional Parliament, the collapse of a state government, unwillingness to use Article 356, ethnic cleansing, continuing violence – what more can this country endure? The hope of the founding fathers and mothers that we will build a multiracial, multireligious, multicultural and multilingual nation where liberty, equality and fraternity will prevail lies in a heap of ruins.

June 30, 2023

PART 4

Law and Legal Matters

I wrote eight essays that have been grouped under 'Law and Legal Matters'. Many of them revolved around decisions of the courts. The intersection of law, politics, social justice and equality is a fascinating subject: I explored the issues that I encountered at the intersection. I did not hesitate to criticise the government or the court. To the best of my knowledge, no one objected to the criticism. My criticism fell under the category of fair criticism.

Blessed Are the Poor (But Not All)

The subject of this essay is at the intersection of law, politics, concept of equality and the idea of social justice.

I have a fairly well-formed position on what is social justice in contemporary India and the way forward. I also have a strong sense of how unequal Indian society is and the hundred things that we have to do to make Indian society more equal. At the intersection of social justice and equality, at times, social justice has suffered and, at other times, equality has been sacrificed.

Laws are made by the legislature which is an assembly, overwhelmingly, of politicians. Laws are administered and applied by judges who are removed from politics. Rulers must fear judges, judges must not fear the rulers. The outcome of the intersection of law and politics is the true measure of whether a country is governed by law or not.

At the Intersection

The judgement of the Supreme Court in *Janhit Abhiyan* delivered on November 7, 2022 is a fine example of the dilemmas that are encountered at the intersection of law, politics, social justice and equality. The judgement was delivered in a batch of cases that challenged the validity of the 103rd Amendment to the Constitution, popularly called the 'EWS reservation case'. EWS stands for economically weaker sections. For this essay, I prefer to call them 'poor'.

I have decided to hold back my view on the judgement and use this essay to lay out the issues and request the reader to take a view.

The Fundamental Issues

There are many kinds of reservations today in educational institutions and government employment. These reservations are for the 'socially and educationally backward classes' which mean the Scheduled Castes (SC), Scheduled Tribes (ST) and Other Backward Classes (OBC). There are historical – and incontrovertible – reasons why these sections of the people are socially and educationally backward. Reservation was considered an instrument of 'affirmative action' and reservations for SCs, STs and OBCs have acquired legitimacy and approval.

These reservations are presumed to have caused 'angst' among sections of the people who do not enjoy any reservation, notably, citizens who are not SC, ST or OBC. The idea was born that the poor among these citizens suffer similar disadvantages in education and employment; so, can a new reservation be carved out for the poor? The idea was conceptually fair but there were obstacles:

- Can the poor be considered 'socially and educationally backward' which is the only category recognised by the Constitution of India for providing reservation?
- Will reservation for the poor to advance economic justice violate the 'basic structure' of the Constitution?
- Since, by judge-made law, all reservations together cannot exceed 50 per cent of the 'seats' or 'jobs', will not a new reservation of 10 per cent breach that ceiling?

The doctrine of 'basic structure' and the principle of a '50 per cent ceiling' are traceable to judgements that interpreted the Constitution. Once the Honourable Judges decided to shed the inhibitions created by judge-made law, the path forward was clear. All five Honourable Judges agreed that economic justice is on the same plane as social justice and that a new reservation based on economic criteria would not violate the basic structure of the Constitution. They also agreed that exceeding the ceiling of 50 per cent in this case was not unconstitutional. They unanimously upheld reservation based on economic criteria and the quantum of 10 per cent. Criticism of this part of the judgement is muted. The issue that has divided opinion is whether the reservation can exclude the poor among the SC, ST and OBC.

The Divided Court

Poverty is the main cause of deficiencies in nutrition, nurturing and early learning. These deficiencies limit or deny access to education and employment. The question that arises is: who are the poor? The 103rd Constitutional Amendment had left it to the states to notify the poor based on 'family income and other indicators of economic disadvantage'. The minority judgement cited the Sinho Commission (July 2010) which had concluded that 31.7 crore people were below the poverty line. Of these, the SC population was 7.74 crore, ST population was 4.25 crore and OBC population was 13.86 crore, totalling 25.85 crore or 81.5 per cent of the BPL population. These proportions among the BPL population could not have changed significantly since 2010.

The crucial question is whether Article 15(6) and Article 16(6) that exclude the poor among the SC, ST and OBC from the new reservation are constitutionally valid. On this issue, the Honourable Judges were divided 3:2. Mr Justice Ravindra Bhat wrote a powerful dissent in which Chief Justice Lalit concurred. His words, 'Our Constitution does not speak the language of exclusion' will reverberate in the court halls of the Supreme Court for many years. In my view, the dissent is 'an appeal to the brooding spirit of the law, to the intelligence of a future day, when a later decision may possibly correct the error' (per Chief Justice Charles Evans Hughes).

Reflect on these possible conclusions: To create a new reservation for the poor will advance economic justice. But to exclude the poor among the SC, ST and OBC (constituting approximately 81.5 per cent of the total poor) from the reservation will deny equality and justice to the poorest among the poor.

November 13, 2022

Hard Talk, Hard Times

Here is an exchange of views (as reported in the newspapers) between a Bench of the Hon'ble Supreme Court and the Union law minister:

> SC: The Centre is frustrating the appointment process of judges in higher judiciary by not clearing names recommended by the Collegium.
>
> LM: Never say that the government is sitting on the files, then don't send the files to the government, you appoint yourself, you run the show.
>
> SC: Let them give the power. We have no difficulty … when somebody high enough says let them do it themselves, we will do it ourselves, no difficulty.

There are profound – I hesitate to say bitter – differences between the Supreme Court and the Executive on the interpretation of Articles 124(2) and 217(1) of the Constitution of India. Under the original provisions, the power of appointment was vested solely in the Executive to be exercised in consultation with the Supreme Court and the High Court concerned. For 40 years, the practice was that the state government would consult the High Court concerned and recommend names to the Central government that would follow the procedure in Article 217 and appoint judges to the High Court. Similarly, the Central government would propose names and, following the procedure in Article 124, appoint judges to the Supreme Court. Many distinguished judges were appointed by the Executive; some bad apples also found a place in the courts.

Reversing Constitution

The practice was reversed by judicial interpretation in the *Second Judges Case* (1993) and the *Third Judges Case* (1998). A new mechanism called the Collegium was invented. The Collegium took over the power of selection of judges for the Supreme Court and the High Courts. The Central government may accept or return the recommendation. If the recommendation was reiterated, the government was obliged to make the appointment. It cannot be said that the quality of judges who have been appointed under the new procedure has been superior to the quality of judges appointed in the first 40 years. Many distinguished judges were appointed but some bad apples were also selected and appointed.

Every government in office since 1993 has bristled against the altered procedure. However, stalling appointments has become a regular practice under the Narendra Modi government. It has also stalled recommendations reiterated by the Collegium which, as two Hon'ble Judges pointed out, was contrary to the law declared by the Supreme Court. As a result, there are seven vacancies in the Supreme Court and 381 vacancies among the 1,108 sanctioned posts of judges in the High Courts (as on July 1, 2022). The greater tragedy has been that meritorious lawyers declined to be considered for judgeship or withdrew the name if the appointment had been stalled for months.

Idea Stillborn

The National Judicial Appointments Commission (NJAC) was created under an Act of Parliament to give equal weight to the judiciary and the Executive in the matter of appointment of judges. There were a few wrinkles in the law that could have been easily ironed out but neither side made the effort. On October 16, 2015, the Supreme Court struck down the Constitution (Ninety-Ninth Amendment) Act, 2014 and with it the National Judicial Commission Act also perished. (The dissenting judgement of Justice Chelameswar is as important as the majority judgement).

In my essay 'Across the Aisle: The NJAC Conundrum' (*Indian Express* on November 1, 2015) I criticised the judgement vehemently, but I also suggested a common ground to make a new law. The strongest arguments on the side of the Executive are that in no other country of the world do judges select new judges and the Executive is best placed to assess the character and suitability of the potential judge. The strongest argument on the side of the judiciary is that serving judges know best about the practising lawyers and serving district judges who alone are qualified to be elevated to the Bench. There is a large dose of truth in both arguments.

If the stand-off continues, the situation will only get worse. There will be more vacancies. More vacancies will mean more, not less, difficulty in filling them. There will be more 'declines' and 'withdrawals'. The legal system, already under considerable strain, will collapse. None will be sadder than the judges, none will be happier than the Executive. The losers will be the people of India, especially those knocking on the doors of the courts seeking justice.

Possible Solution

I believe that the Executive cannot be totally excluded from the process of selecting potential judges. I also believe, given the current state of partisan, vindictive and majoritarian politics, the Executive cannot be entrusted with the sole power to select potential judges. Both judiciary and Executive must find a place in NJAC 2.0. In my essay, I had suggested that the Collegium may have the exclusive power to propose/nominate candidates; the NJAC may have the power to select and recommend; and the Executive may have the power (coupled with a duty) to appoint. The procedure can be refined further if the task is entrusted to a few non-judge legal luminaries.

The rising number of vacancies in the courts – and common sense – requires that the Executive and the judiciary must display a degree of statesmanship to resolve the issue. Absent statesmanship, hard words will become harsh words, the wounds will continue to fester and justice will be the casualty.

December 4, 2022

Constitutional Authorities vs Constitution

The quote has been attributed to Edmund Burke, George Santayana and Winston Churchill. The version that is often quoted is: 'Those who cannot remember the past are condemned to repeat it.' Karl Marx's variation carried more punch. He said, 'History repeats itself, first as a tragedy, then as a farce.'

In recent weeks, three constitutional authorities have occupied centre stage: Mr Jagdeep Dhankhar, Hon'ble Vice President of India and Chairman, Rajya Sabha, born 1951; Mr Om Birla, Hon'ble Speaker, Lok Sabha, born 1962; and Mr Kiren Rijiju, Hon'ble Minister of Law and Justice, born 1971. The first would have experienced the days of the Emergency (1975–1977), the second would have heard and read about it, and the third, given the office he holds now, would have studied its history.

In 1967, in an unremarkable property dispute, *Golaknath vs State of Punjab*, the Supreme Court held (by a majority of 6:5) that the fundamental rights contained in Part III of the Constitution of India could not be abrogated or abridged by Parliament. The central issue was 'property', not 'freedom'. Therefore, the debate became ideological.

Unalterable Features

The judgement in *Kesavananda Bharati vs State of Kerala* (1973) contained nothing that should have caused alarm. The central issue was, again, 'property'. The Court upheld the

Kerala Land Reforms Act and the petitioner lost the case. The Court also upheld the power of Parliament to amend the Constitution, including the fundamental rights, save the basic structure of the Constitution. The few examples of the 'basic structure' that the Court noted were beyond controversy. Who can find fault with the conclusion that federalism, secularism and an independent judiciary are basic features of the Constitution? The debate continued, but it was less ideological than the debate stirred by Golaknath.

The immediate cause of the Emergency proclaimed on June 25, 1975 was an event unrelated to Parliament's power to amend the Constitution. It was the annulment of the election of Prime Minister Indira Gandhi by an election tribunal. Nani Palkhivala had accepted the brief on behalf of Indira Gandhi and I am certain he would have succeeded in overturning the judgement in a regular appeal to the Supreme Court. However, in an egregious overreach, a number of steps were taken, including constitutional amendments, that would have turned India into an authoritarian and repressive state.

The only bulwark was the judiciary. Truth be told, the judiciary failed the people. The lowest point in the history of the Supreme Court was the *ADM Jabalpur* case. Justice H.R. Khanna alone stood up to the onslaught on the liberties enshrined in the Constitution. In the High Courts, thankfully, there were some judges who refused to abide by the judgement of the Supreme Court and upheld personal liberty, notably Justices J.S. Verma and R.K. Tankha in Madhya Pradesh.

Conflating Two Issues

I believe that Mr Dhankhar, Mr Birla and Mr Rijiju have read the history of the period from 1967 to 1977.

Mr Dhankhar is conflating two separate issues. Whether Parliament can amend every and any provision of the Constitution and whether that is beyond the pale of judicial review is one issue. Whether the judgement of the Supreme Court striking down the 99th Constitutional Amendment and the National Judicial Appointments Commission Act was correct is a different issue. One can hold the view that *Kesavananda Bharati* was correctly decided and hold the view that the NJAC case was wrongly decided. Many legal scholars hold those views.

Unfortunately, the debate sparked by Mr Dhankhar has spawned many questions that are critical to the idea of India as a federal, democratic republic. Mr Rijiju has made the confusion worse by wading into the debate with a demand for a seat for the government in the Collegium system that he wishes to abolish! The alarm bells have begun to ring that a sinister plan is in the making to 'overhaul' the Constitution.

Answer Questions

Suppose we concede parliamentary supremacy over the Constitution. Let me ask a few questions:

Would you agree if a State is dismembered and multiple Union Territories are carved out (a la Jammu and Kashmir)?

Would you agree if freedom of speech, freedom to reside in any part of India, and freedom to practice any profession or carry on any business is abolished?

Would you approve of a law that will treat men and women unequally; treat Hindu and non-Hindu differently; or deny rights to LGBTQ+?

Would you agree if the rights guaranteed to Muslims, Christians, Sikhs, Parsis, Jains, Buddhists, Jews and other minorities under the Constitution are abolished?

Would you agree if List II (State List) was removed from the Seventh Schedule and all legislative power concentrated in Parliament?

Would you agree if learning a particular language was made compulsory for all Indians?

Would you approve of a law that stipulated every person accused of an offence shall be presumed to be guilty until he/she is proven to be innocent?

Today, Parliament cannot make such laws. They will be subject to judicial review. On the contrary, under the doctrine of 'Parliamentary Supremacy and Judicial Forbearance', such laws cannot be reviewed or struck down by the courts.

Fifty years after the verdict, *Kesavananda Bharati* is being portrayed as a ghost that haunts India and inhibits our progress. I believe it is an angel that guards the country, the Constitution and the people.

January 22, 2023

Might and Plight on Display

Act I: Might

Mr Kiren Rijiju, Honourable Minister of Law and Justice, uses every opportunity to emphasise that he and his government do not interfere – and have never interfered – with the independence of the judiciary. As a citizen and a practising advocate, I would like to believe him. I was happy to hear Mr Rijiju restate the position of the government in a recent interaction at the India Today Conclave.

Midway, he delivered a thunderbolt. He said, and I shall quote his words:

> I feel this is the most important topic for me, for the nation. … There is a calibrated effort to undermine Indian judiciary. That is why they say, day in and day out, they are saying that government is trying to take over Indian judiciary. … In a way, it is a sinister design … The anti-India forces in India and outside India, they use same language … The same eco-system is working inside India and outside India also … We will not allow this tukde tukde gang to destroy India's integrity and our sovereignty …
>
> Recently, there was one seminar in Delhi. Some retired Supreme Court judges, some senior lawyers, some people were there. The topic of the seminar was 'Accountability in Judges Appointment'. But the discussion whole day was on 'how government is taking over the Indian judiciary'… it is a few of the retired judges, few maybe three or four, few of those activists, part of the anti-India

> gang, these people are trying to make Indian judiciary play the role of Opposition party …
>
> Actions will be taken, actions are being taken as per law, but if I say that I will take action … The agencies will take action as per the provisions of the law. Nobody will escape, don't worry, nobody will escape. Those who work against the country will have to pay a price for that …

It was an unambiguous statement. What was on display was the might of the State through its law minister, no less. The mighty State was saying that if the government comes to the conclusion, *subjectively*, that there is a tukde tukde gang or that any person is part of the anti-India gang, be forewarned that action will be taken against anyone who *speaks or plays the role of the Opposition*. We know who the 'agencies' are. We know what action they will take. We know what price the person will pay. We also know that the process is the punishment.

Many have criticised the statement of the Honourable Minister of Law and Justice and its chilling effect on free speech. In my view, it was a display of the raw power of the State and provides sufficient evidence that democracy is in danger.

Act II: Plight

Move over to another organ of the State: the judiciary. At the apex of the judiciary sits the Supreme Court of India, sometimes described as the most powerful court in the world. On March 21, 2023, a three-judge Bench delivered a judgement in the case of *Satender Kumar Antil vs Central Bureau of Investigation*. Noting its earlier judgement in the same case passed in July 2022 on the issue of 'bail', the Court said, and I shall quote its words:

> Counsels have produced before us a bunch of orders passed in breach of the judgement in the case of *Satender Kumar Antil vs CBI & Anr* only as samples to show how at the ground level, despite almost 10 months passing, there are a number of aberrations … This is something which cannot be countenanced and, in our view, it is the duty of the High Courts to ensure that the subordinate judiciary under their supervision follows the law of the land. If such orders are being passed by some Magistrates, it may even require judicial work to be withdrawn and those Magistrates to be sent to the judicial academies for upgradation of their skills for some time.
>
> Another aspect which is sought to be pointed out … is that not only is there a duty of the Court but also of the public prosecutors to plead correct legal position before the Court as officers of the Court.

Just as 'free speech' is guaranteed under Article 19(1)(a) of the Constitution of India, 'liberty' is guaranteed under Articles 19 and 21. Both are basic, unalterable features of a democracy. The anguish expressed by the Supreme Court illustrates the plight of the law caught in the middle between overbearing investigating agencies and an indulgent subordinate judiciary (with notable exceptions).

Act III: Might and Plight

On March 23, 2023 Mr Rahul Gandhi was convicted by a magistrate's court on a complaint (by a BJP functionary) of the offence of defamation under Sections 499 and 500, IPC for certain words uttered during a political campaign/ interview. He was convicted and sentenced to two years' imprisonment. The lawyers representing Mr Gandhi have found fault with the judgement of the learned magistrate on grounds of lack of jurisdiction, procedural errors and manifest injustice. They also viewed the punishment of two years' imprisonment (the maximum under the law) as unusually harsh. Robust political discourse is the essence of democracy. On deeper analysis, it will be evident that the law was set in motion to silence a leading voice of the democratic Opposition. Noisy appreciation of the 'might' of the law must be tempered by calm introspection on the 'plight' of democratic voices.

March 26, 2023

Law May Stumble, Justice Will Triumph

Courts are established to deliver justice according to law. Sometimes, justice may stumble, but litigants in India can reasonably hope that if they continue the journey on the tortuous path, they will get justice, *eventually*. With that preface, I shall explain a case that has caught the attention of the whole country and stirred passions on either side of the political divide.

On March 23, 2023 a magistrate in Gujarat convicted Mr Rahul Gandhi of the offence of defamation (Section 499, IPC) and imposed a sentence of imprisonment of 2 years. After pronouncing the sentence, the magistrate suspended the sentence. Nonetheless, on March 24, Mr Gandhi was disqualified and his seat in the Lok Sabha was declared vacant.

Here is the path the case travelled:

13-04-2019: Mr Gandhi made an election speech in Kolar, Karnataka

16-04-2019: Mr Purnesh Modi, MLA (BJP), filed a complaint before a magistrate in Surat, Gujarat, that Mr Gandhi had defamed the entire Modi community

07-03-2022: Complainant sought and obtained a stay of the trial of his own complaint from the High Court, Gujarat

07-02-2023: Mr Gandhi spoke in the Lok Sabha on the Adani Group's issues

16-02-2023: Complainant withdrew his petition before the High Court, Gujarat
21-02-2023: Trial resumed before the magistrate
17-03-2023: Trial concluded, judgement reserved
23-03-2023: Magistrate delivered a 168-page judgement, found Mr Gandhi guilty, imposed a sentence of two years' imprisonment. Shortly thereafter, the magistrate suspended the sentence
24-03-2023: Lok Sabha Secretariat notified the disqualification of Mr Gandhi

A routine case that meandered for three years, suddenly acquired urgency and surged forward at lightning speed from resumption of trial to conviction in 30 days. The puzzle is, what imparted the urgency? Why did the complainant obtain a stay of the trial of his own complaint and why did he, nine days after Mr Gandhi spoke in the Lok Sabha, withdraw his petition and seek immediate resumption of the stalled trial?

Who Was Defamed?

The complainant alleged that the Modi community/ caste, to which he belonged, was defamed. Frankly, I do not know whether there is a community called 'Modi' or if everyone with the surname 'Modi' belonged to one community or caste. The *Indian Express* has explained (March 28, 2023) that the word Modi 'does not denote any specific community or caste. In Gujarat, the Modi surname is used by Hindus, Muslims and Parsis. There are people with the Modi surname among Vaishnavas (Baniyas), Kharwas (fishermen) from Porbandar, and Lohanas (who are a community of traders).' The newspaper also found that there is no community or caste by the name 'Modi' in the Central list of OBCs.

Also, there is no 'Modi' in the Central list for Bihar or Rajasthan. In the Central list for Gujarat, there is 'Modi Ghanchi'. For me, who had forsworn caste six decades ago and does not recognise caste, the entire argument of defaming a community/caste (allegedly 13 crore–strong) makes the head spin.

Punishment, Sentence Suspended

According to the complaint, it was a case of slander. Under IPC Section 500, the punishment may extend to imprisonment for two years, or with fine, or with both. I know of no case since 1860 (when the IPC came into force) where the maximum sentence of imprisonment for two years was imposed in a case of slander. Ordinarily, where a sentence of imprisonment for three years or less is imposed, the accused is granted bail so that he is a free person to seek relief from a higher court against the conviction and sentence. However, in this case, within minutes of imposing the sentence, the magistrate himself suspended the sentence.

Section 8(3) of the Representation of the People Act, 1951, provides that 'A person convicted of any offence and sentenced to imprisonment for not less than two years … shall be disqualified from the date of such conviction …'

In the case of Mr Gandhi there is a conviction but no sentence that is effective or operating. Therefore, did he incur a disqualification on March 23, 2023? It is a moot question. Many have asked the question and are looking for an answer. However, the powers that be had no doubt whatsoever. Within 24 hours, whether they had asked the question or not and whether they had found the answer or not, the Lok Sabha Secretariat disqualified Mr Gandhi.

Who Can Disqualify?

Article 102(2)(e) of the Constitution of India provides that a person '*shall be disqualified* ... for being a member ... if he is disqualified by or under any law made by Parliament'. Be it noted that the words used are not '*shall stand disqualified*' but '*shall be disqualified*', implying that an order of disqualification will be necessary. The obvious question has been asked (by among others Mr P.D.T. Achary, former secretary general of the Lok Sabha), who has the authority to disqualify? Article 103 may contain the answer: it says, 'if any question arises... the question shall be referred for the decision of the President' who 'shall obtain the opinion of the Election Commission and shall act according to such opinion'. In Mr Gandhi's case, the question was not referred to the President; nor did the Election Commission offer any opinion. So, who took the decision? Was it the Hon'ble Speaker or a body known as the Lok Sabha Secretariat? No one knows.

Adapting Winston Churchill, the case and its outcomes so far are riddles wrapped in a mystery.

April 2, 2023

Prosecutor, Jury and Judge

Old Ramanathapuram district in Tamil Nadu (now divided into three: Ramanathapuram, Sivagangai and Virudhunagar) is a district with multiple waterbodies – natural lakes, man-made tanks, irrigation tanks (kanmois, in Tamil), drinking water ponds (oorani), tanks for cattle and sheep and for washing (kulam), and wells. Old Ramanathapuram was a dry-land district that received little rain. Most agricultural land was unirrigated and monsoon-dependent. The people and their rulers had no choice but to dig and dig and dig, and create waterbodies. They did that round the year. The waterbodies were the lifeline for both people and animals.

As the population grew and new human settlements became imperative, the casualty was the waterbody. The time-tested tactic was 'creeping encroachments'. A few huts will spring up on the edges of a waterbody; more will be erected in the following months. As encroachments spread, the waterbody began to recede, until one day it vanished. Like when the sea advanced, the coastline receded. It is called erosion.

No Snatching, but Erosion

The two words – encroachment and erosion – apply to freedom too. In a free country, freedom will not be snatched at midnight. It will be eroded – silently, furtively, insidiously – until you know one day that you are no longer as free as you were some months ago. And when you realise that you have lost your freedom, it will be too late to retrieve what you have lost.

Don't live under the illusion that you cannot lose your freedom. Just count the nations that got freedom at about the same time as India did in 1947 and in the following decade. And now count how many of them have lost their freedom not to colonisers but to native autocrats. Many of those countries still have an Election Commission and elections; a judiciary and judges; a parliament and MPs; a cabinet and ministers; and newspapers and journalists. But when you visit the country or live in it, you know it is not a free country. Such countries have the trappings of a free country, but they are authoritarian states. The V-Dem Institute of Sweden classifies countries as liberal democracy, electoral democracy, electoral autocracy and closed autocracy. In 2021, the Institute classified India as an 'electoral autocracy'. It is a badge of shame.

Successive Amendments

Articles 14 and 19(1)(a) and (g) of the Constitution protect the freedoms of the individual as well as of the institution called the Press. Mark April 6, 2023. It was the day on which the erosion of freedom of the Press got the sanction of a doubtful law. During the Emergency (1975–1977), freedom of the Press was snatched overnight. (It was terribly wrong and Indira Gandhi apologised for the Emergency.) On April 6, the government amended the Information Technology Rules, 2021. Rule 3(1)(b)(v), after amendment, reads as follows (the amendment is in italics).

> 3(1) Due diligence by an intermediary: An intermediary, including a social media intermediary, a significant

> social media intermediary and an online gaming intermediary, shall observe the following due diligence while discharging its duties, namely:
>
> (b) the intermediary shall … make reasonable efforts to cause the user of its computer resource not to host, display, upload, modify, publish, transmit, store, update or share any information that, … deceives or misleads the addressee about the origin of the message or knowingly and intentionally communicates any misinformation or information which is patently false and untrue or misleading in nature *or, in respect of any business of the Central Government, is identified as fake or false or misleading by such fact check unit of the Central Government as the Ministry may, by notification published in the Official Gazette, specify*.

The mischief is obvious. The amended rule applies to 'any business of the Central Government'. There will be a 'fact check unit of the central government'. That is a euphemism for an Official Censor. The censor is empowered to identify the news as 'fake or false'. That decision will be purely subjective with no judicial oversight. Once the news is identified as fake or false, newspapers, TV channels and social media outlets shall 'cause the user of its computer resource' to remove the news.

Before It Is Gone

I shall not burden this essay with the screaming legal infirmities in the amended rule. Suffice to say, the government is the prosecutor, jury and judge of what is fake/false and what is not.

The amended rule has a history. The Information Technology Rules made in 2021 imposed onerous obligations on intermediaries. The Rules have been challenged in various courts. On October 28, 2022, the government notified the Information Technology (Intermediary Guidelines and Digital Media Ethics Code) Rules, 2022 and made the first significant amendment to Rule 3(1)b)(v). Now, the notification of April 6, 2023 has further amended Rule 3(1)(b)(v). This is what I call creeping erosion of freedom.

Let the courts decide whether the amended Rules are legal or not under the Constitution and the laws. You must look at the non-legal and freedom-related aspects:

- Should news be censored in a free, democratic country?
- Would you accept a censor of news?
- Should the censor be a government-appointed censor?
- Should the censor decide the question subjectively?
- Will such government action not create a 'chilling effect' on freedom of speech and expression?

A precious right is being eroded. It is going, going … Wake up before it is gone.

April 16, 2023

Which Law, Whose Order?

The Constitution of India was in the making for over two years and it came into effect on January 26, 1950. It was the product of the collective wisdom of the Constituent Assembly which was reasonably, though not fully, representative of the people of India. In popular imagination, the Constitution's soul is attributed to Babasaheb Ambedkar.

The Indian Penal Code – the backbone of the body of criminal laws of India – was made in 1860 during British rule. It has passed the test of many British-made 'basic laws' and the Constitution of India; it has also survived many amendments. The companion laws are the Indian Evidence Act, 1872 and the Code of Criminal Procedure, 1973. All three laws were passed by the central legislature/ Parliament and can be amended or added to by the state legislature.

What Is Law and Order?

Under the Constitution, the subjects of 'criminal law' and 'criminal procedure' are included in the Seventh Schedule, List III-Concurrent List. However, the subject of 'public order' that includes 'law and order' is allotted to the state legislature under List II-State List. Executive power in relation to public order is also vested in the state government (Article 162). Such a power carries with it a duty to enforce the law which means applying the laws, preventing the violation of the laws, apprehending suspects, investigation, prosecution, and securing conviction and punishment of the accused – *in accordance with law and lawful orders.*

Recent events have given rise to the suspicion that the phrase 'law and order' may have been infused with perverse meanings. It seems 'law' is no longer enacted law, it is 'law' as *understood and applied* by the law enforcers. Further, 'order' no longer means a lawful order, but includes *oral or non-verbal instructions* issued by persons who have assumed arbitrary power. Whenever 'law and order' is invoked, I am tempted to ask 'Which law?' and 'Whose order?'

Universal Principles

Law is premised on certain universal legal and moral principles. Worldwide, in democratic countries, the following presumptions in law are considered inviolable:

- Every person is presumed innocent until proven guilty in a court of law.
- No person shall be deprived of his life or personal liberty except according to procedure established by law (Article 21).
- Criminal law is written law: it includes laws creating offences and laws laying down the procedure for registration, investigation, prosecution and trial of offences, and punishment thereof.
- The accused must be tried in an open court of competent jurisdiction.
- The accused has the right to defend himself and plead his case in person or through a pleader.
- The prosecutor is an officer of the court and must fairly disclose all the material, whether they are in favour of the investigating agency or in favour of the accused.

- The judge alone has the jurisdiction to determine whether the accused is guilty of the offence or not and, if found guilty, to impose a punishment.

If these universal principles are not observed, could it be called a country governed by the rule *of* law? Some countries follow the system 'show me the person and I'll show you the rule'. It is a system where there is no rule of law but it is claimed there is rule *by* law and that is sufficient. Under that system, the law may be different from person to person, case to case, and even day to day. The stark difference between rule of law and rule by law is self-evident; yet, increasingly, the difference is either deliberately not noticed or is being erased. On orders that may – or do – violate the law, many errant law-enforcing officers adopt the Adolf Eichmann justification, *Befehl ist Befehl* (command is command).

Acts of Impunity

Enough of legal philosophy. Let's face the hard reality.

- Pehlu Khan, a dairy farmer, was transporting cattle bought at a fair. He was assaulted by cow vigilantes on the Jaipur–Delhi highway. The attack was captured on video. He died in the hospital. Two years later, the six accused persons were acquitted giving them the benefit of doubt. Moments later, their supporters raised slogans of 'Bharat Mata ki Jai'.
- Over 300 incidents of attacks on Christian churches and prayer meetings have been reported every year from Odisha, Uttar Pradesh, Jharkhand, Chhattisgarh, Gujarat, Karnataka, etc. According to ANI, after a UP law of 2020 against conversion came into force, 507 persons have been accused of 'conversion' but none convicted so far.

- Accusing Muslim men of luring and trapping Hindu women into marrying them, cases of 'love jihad' have been filed across many states. In February 2020, the minister of state (home) told Parliament that 'love jihad' is not defined under the law and no such case has been reported by any of the central agencies. In December 2022, the Vishwa Hindu Parishad released a list of 400 so-called love jihad cases.
- On March 26, Atiq Ahmed, a prisoner accused of many crimes, shouted to journalists that he would be killed in an 'encounter'. On April 16, Atiq Ahmed and his brother, Ashraf, were killed while being escorted by the police to a hospital in Allahabad (Prayagraj). The assailants shouted Jai Shri Ram, threw down their guns and surrendered. A week earlier, Atiq Ahmed's son was killed in an 'encounter' with the UP police. According to the *Indian Express*, it was the 183rd encounter after Mr Adityanath became chief minister of Uttar Pradesh. Many people said that 'god had delivered justice'.

Which *law* authorised such killings, attacks and excesses? Under whose *orders* were the victims killed or churches attacked or cases filed against couples? And finally, why bring Bharat Mata, Lord Ram and god into the seemingly inexorable perversion of the *rule of law*?

April 23, 2023

Reform (Not Uniform) Personal Laws

The Constitution of India has a whole chapter on Directive Principles of State Policy pertaining to the welfare of citizens. Article 44 is one among 18 articles of Chapter IV which contains the Directive Principles. From the point of view of equality and non-discrimination, the directive in Article 38(2) to minimise the inequalities in income and to eliminate inequalities in status, facilities and opportunities is important. The directive in Article 39 is a central pillar of the chapter from the point of view of social and economic justice. Article 43 directs the State to secure a 'living wage' and is the aspiration of millions belonging to the working classes.

Sadly, there is hardly any debate on these Directive Principles. They are not on the government's agenda. Article 44 alone has occupied much of the political space, thanks to the agenda of the RSS–BJP and some observations of the Supreme Court.

Words Have Meaning

Let's look at the language of Article 44: 'The State shall endeavour to secure for the citizens a uniform civil code throughout the territory of India.' Words have meaning. Unlike Humpty Dumpty's answer to Alice, a word does not mean 'what I choose it to mean'. 'Uniform' is not 'common'. 'Shall endeavour to secure' is not 'shall secure'. Babasaheb Ambedkar and his colleagues were not ignoramuses. They had a deep knowledge and understanding of the history, religions, caste differences, social and family systems, cultural practices and customs of the Indian people, and they chose the words of Chapter IV carefully.

Uniform Civil Code is shorthand for personal laws. It concerns laws in four areas: Marriage and Divorce, Succession and Inheritance, Minority and Guardianship, and Adoption and Maintenance. Over the centuries, the personal laws of different sections of the people and different geographical areas of the country have evolved in different ways. Who ruled the people played an important part in the evolution. Religion played a crucial part while geography, fertility, conquest, migration, and foreign influences also impacted personal laws.

Reforms Started in 1955

As personal laws stand today, there is gender discrimination as well as non-gender-based discrimination, some unscientific and unhealthy practices as well as reprehensible practices and customs. Undoubtedly, these aspects of personal laws need to be reformed.

Reform of personal laws is not new. It has been on the national agenda since the making of the Constitution. It was among the top concerns of the first Parliament of India (1952–57). Among the champions of reform were Jawaharlal Nehru and Babasaheb Ambedkar. Four major laws were passed amending and codifying the Hindu law braving the opposition of orthodox and conservative sections of the people: the Hindu Marriage Act, 1955; Hindu Succession Act, 1956; Hindu Minority and Guardianship Act, 1956; and Hindu Adoptions and Maintenance Act, 1956.

A young nation did a remarkable job of reforming the personal laws of the majority Hindu community.

It was revolutionary, but the revolution allowed some aspects to remain. Not all discriminatory provisions were removed; the Hindu Undivided Family, as a legal entity, was acknowledged; and custom and usage in marriage were recognised as exceptions. The last aspect is crucial because most marriages in India are solemnised according to custom.

More amendments were made in 1961, 1962, 1964, 1976, 1978, 1999, 2001 and 2003. Between 2005 and 2008, another set of reforms was made by the UPA government. Three of the four Acts (listed above) were amended. The revolutionary change was conferring equal property rights on daughters and sons. New laws, namely, the Protection of Women from Domestic Violence Act, 2005, the Prohibition of Child Marriage Act, 2006 and the Maintenance and Welfare of Parents and Senior Citizens Act, 2007 were passed. Courts stepped in where the legislative bodies hesitated. On August 22, 2017, the Supreme Court struck down the practice of talaq-e-bidat (triple talaq) among Muslims as unconstitutional.

Heed the 21st Law Commission

We paused when we faced the personal laws of the tribal people. None of the four Acts (listed above) apply to the Scheduled Tribes notified under Article 366, clause 25 of the Constitution. The Sixth Schedule of the Constitution was added for the administration of tribal areas in Assam, Meghalaya, Tripura and Mizoram and included a paragraph conferring powers on District Councils and Regional Councils in those states to make laws with respect to inheritance, marriage and divorce, and social customs. Special provisions protecting the religious or social practices and customary law were added for Nagaland (Article 371A), Sikkim (Article 371F) and Mizoram (Article

371G). A demand for similar special provisions has been raised by tribal bodies in Chhattisgarh and Jharkhand.

More reforms in personal laws are certainly necessary. The 21st Law Commission gave sage advice: 'This Commission has, therefore, dealt with laws that are discriminatory rather than providing a UCC which is neither necessary nor desirable at this stage … Cultural diversity cannot be compromised to the extent that our urge for uniformity itself becomes a threat to the territorial integrity of the country.'

The Hon'ble Prime Minister has framed the issue in a manner permitting only a binary response – for or against the Uniform Civil Code. This approach treats the people of India as dumb driven sheep. A nuanced approach will be to start a meaningful conversation on the reforms that need to be made in all personal laws, Muslim law included. The keyword is reform, not uniform.

July 9, 2023

Equality, Adversity and Diversity

Harvard College, founded in 1636, is the core of Harvard University. New schools/colleges have been added in the last four centuries, but the pride of place is occupied by Harvard College that offers graduate and postgraduate courses.

For good reason: over 60,000 students applied in 2022, fewer than 2,000 were admitted. As the US Supreme Court noted, 'Harvard is thus no easy feat. It can depend on having excellent grades, glowing recommendation letters, or overcoming significant adversity. It can also depend on your race.'

Earlier, the contest was between white Americans and black Americans. When I was admitted to Harvard Business School, in a class of about 750, there was a sprinkling of black Americans, a handful of Asians (four of Indian origin) and a couple of Africans. But America has changed dramatically. The battle for admission is now fought by whites, blacks, Asians, Hispanics, Africans and students from the Middle East. The latest court battle was instituted by Students For Fair Admission, Inc. against the President and Fellows of Harvard College. The second case was against the University of North Carolina (UNC), another old university. In a typical year, UNC receives 43,500 applications and admits 4,200 in the freshman class.

Adversity vs Equality

The central issue in the two cases was whether race (an adverse factor) can be considered as a relevant criterion for selection. That issue has troubled America since the 13 British colonies declared their independence on July 4, 1776. The issue led to the Civil War (1861–1865).

The issue of race versus constitutional guarantee of equality has engaged the US Supreme Court since 1896. The issue was tested on the anvil of the Fourteenth Amendment to the US Constitution that reads:

> No State shall make or enforce any law which shall abridge the privileges or immunities of citizens of the United States; nor shall any State deprive any person of life, liberty, or property, without due process of law; nor deny to any person within its jurisdiction the equal protection of the laws.

These fundamental rights were incorporated, almost verbatim, in Articles 14 and 21 of the Constitution of India.

The history of the Fourteenth Amendment reflects the history and evolution of race relations between white and black Americans. In 1896, the US Supreme Court propounded the theory of 'separate but equal'. It was reversed in 1954 in *Brown vs Board of Education* which held that 'separate cannot be equal'.

Racially discriminatory laws were subjected to 'strict scrutiny' and allowed to stand only when there was a 'compelling governmental interest' and the use of race was 'narrowly tailored'. In two subsequent decisions – *Regents of University of California vs Bakke* (1978) and *Grutter vs Bollinger* (2003) – the court affirmed the view that 'student body diversity is a compelling state interest that can justify the use of race in university admissions'. The court also deferred to the universities' judgement on selection of students.

After 20 years, the above statement of law has been overturned. The irony is that the law has been rewritten not at the instance of the majority white Americans but at the instance of a student body that claimed to represent other minorities, especially Asian Americans!

Republican vs Democrat

The Harvard and the University of North Carolina cases were decided by a majority of six justices to three. They have been labelled as Conservatives and Liberals. The six 'conservative' judges (Chief Justice John Roberts and Justices Thomas, Alito, Gorusch, Kavanaugh and Barrett) were appointed by Republican presidents. The three 'liberal' judges (Justices Sotomayor, Kagan and Jackson) were appointed by Democratic presidents. Superficially, it is conservative vs liberal judges; in reality it is Republican-appointed vs Democrat-appointed judges.

By the same majority of 6:3, in *Planned Parenthood vs Casey*, the US Supreme Court overturned *Roe vs Wade* (1973) that had declared the right of a woman to abort her child. Polls show that 60 per cent of Americans disapprove of the decision in *Casey*.

The judgement in the Harvard and the University of North Carolina cases illustrates the danger of conferring the power to select judges on the political executive. A President whose party controls the Senate can appoint any one as a Judge as long as the nominee shares the ideology of the President's political party. Thrown out of the window are the fundamental principles of the Constitution, Constitutional history and morality, precedents, evolution of public opinion and, above all, current ethos and wishes of the majority of the people.

Judges' Predispositions

There is a lesson for India. Reverting to the earlier pre-Collegium position of empowering the Executive (prime minister) to select judges of the Supreme Court and the High Courts would be dangerous in a highly polarised nation.

Reserving the power exclusively to the Collegium is equally unacceptable because the five judges of the Collegium have their preferences and predispositions. It may be rare that an undeserving judge was appointed to the higher judiciary but there are numerous cases of eminently deserving persons who were overlooked or the recommendations of the Collegium were rejected by the government or inordinately delayed. Besides, diversity and representation on the court have been major casualties.

Equality is the desired norm, adversity is a harsh reality, diversity is a felt need. To balance the three, we must have a mechanism to select judges which will be faithful to the Fundamental Principles of the Constitution.

July 16, 2023

PART 5

Politics and Political Parties

Some of the essays in this section could have been placed in other sections. Perhaps the editors thought that the essays concerned political parties and political leaders and their actions and behaviour, and deserved to be grouped under one section. I saluted the courage of Ms Kasthuri, a student who stood up to the finance minister of India. I commented on subjects like Hindi and hijab. I described some governors as 'wannabe chief ministers'. Readers will find that no subject was beyond fair and restrained comment.

Azadi, Autonomy and Mr Azad

Since 1947 there have been two opposing ideas of Kashmir. From time to time, the ideas mutated into many variants creating an impression that there were more than two ideas of Kashmir. Actually, there are only two ideas and they oppose each other.

The original idea is embodied in the history of Kashmir and the Instrument of Accession signed by the then Maharaja of Kashmir, Hari Singh, on October 26, 1947. The Constituent Assembly recognised the Instrument of Accession and the Congress party embraced the idea behind it. Although the Congress party diluted its position over the years, it reaffirmed the core of the idea – special status – at every opportunity.

The opposite idea owes its origin to Syama Prasad Mukherjee, who was a member of the first Cabinet of Jawaharlal Nehru in 1947. The RSS and its political offspring, including the BJP, embraced Mukherjee's idea, added layers to it over the years, and distorted it to a point where they rejected the Instrument of Accession.

Congress's Consistent Stand

On August 5, 2019, the BJP government took the extreme step of abrogating the special status of Jammu and Kashmir, dismembered the state and created two union territories – Jammu and Kashmir, and Ladakh.

On the next day, the Congress Working Committee (CWC) convened an emergency meeting and adopted a resolution that, inter alia, read:

> The CWC deplores the unilateral, brazen and totally undemocratic manner in which Article 370 of the Constitution was abrogated and the State of Jammu and Kashmir was dismembered by misinterpreting the provisions of the Constitution ... Article 370 is the Constitutional recognition of the terms of the Instrument of Accession between the State of Jammu and Kashmir and India. It deserved to be honoured until it was amended, after consultation with all sections of the people, and strictly in accordance with the Constitution of India.

Mr Ghulam Nabi Azad, a senior and long-time member of the CWC, was present and voted in favour of the resolution.

Steps Not Irreversible

It is necessary to recall the purportedly 'legal' steps taken by the Modi government:

1. No Constitution (Amendment) Bill was brought in Parliament or passed.
2. On August 5, 2019, the government issued an Order under Article 370(1) superseding a similar Order of 1954 and adding clause (4) to Article 367 (the Interpretation Article of the Constitution).
3. On the same day, the government brought a Resolution before Parliament for the repeal of Article 370 and it was passed by both Houses, purportedly under the proviso to Article 370(3) of the Constitution.

4. On the same day, the government introduced and passed in the Rajya Sabha the Jammu and Kashmir (Re-organization) Bill, 2019 bifurcating the state and creating two union territories. It was passed by the Lok Sabha on the next day. This was done purportedly under Article 3 of the Constitution.
5. On August 6, 2019, the President made a notification purportedly under Article 370(3) of the Constitution declaring that all the clauses of Article 370 shall as from August 6, 2019 cease to be operative except a new sole clause that was introduced by the same notification.

All members of the CWC were convinced that the above steps were illegal and unconstitutional. Nothing that the government did on those two fateful days required a two-thirds majority of the members present and voting in either House. The order and the notification were issued in exercise of executive powers. The resolution and the bill were passed with a simple majority.

These questionable steps have been challenged in the Supreme Court. If the Supreme Court holds any or all of the steps to be unconstitutional, the step(s) will be reversed. Alternatively, if another government replaced the Modi government, it is possible that the new government may reverse some or all of the steps. Mr Azad certainly knows all that. Then, why did Mr Azad say that a political party promising to restore Article 370 would be 'telling lies' to the people (something he would never do)?

Not Azadi, but Autonomy

The issue that is central to the people of Jammu and Kashmir is not Article 370. It is the special status.

Notwithstanding the 'repeal' of Article 370 in August 2019, the vast majority of the people of the Kashmir Valley (and there is significant support in Jammu and Ladakh as well) crave for a special status that, by and large, confers autonomy on the state while Jammu and Kashmir remains, forever, an integral part of the Republic of India. In my numerous interactions with the people, I was convinced that they do not demand Azadi or freedom or secession. They seek a large degree of *autonomy*. They recall the words of P.V. Narasimha Rao ('the sky is the limit') and of A.B. Vajpayee ('insaniyat, jamhuriat, Kashmiriyat'). There is nothing unusual in a state craving a large degree of autonomy within a federation. India continues to recommend that very course to Sri Lanka, as recently as on August 12, 2022 at the United Nations Human Rights Council. The Naga groups demand the same in their talks with the government which are stalled on the issue of 'degree of autonomy'.

Mr Azad, Member, CWC, MP and leader of the Opposition, lent his voice to the original idea of Kashmir. It is an unfortunate turn of fate that Mr Azad, minus the status of MP, has embraced the opposite idea of Kashmir.

September 18, 2022

The Leader and the President

There is an unusual, almost obtrusive, interest in the internal party elections of the Congress party. Two years ago, nobody in India including the BJP rank and file, and certainly no member of the Congress party, cared tuppence when Mr J.P. Nadda was 'elected' president of the BJP. Nobody bothered to ask about the 'electoral rolls'. Nobody knew who the returning officer was or if Mr Nadda had filed his 'nomination'. Although the BJP was the ruling party and boasted of having the 'largest' membership of any political party in the world, Mr Nadda's election was a non-event.

The extraordinary interest shown by the BJP and the media in the Congress party's elections is proof of two facts: one, that Congress-mukt India is a myth and a mirage – it will never happen – and two, that the Bharat Jodo Yatra has shaken the BJP out of its complacency and has made the media, otherwise dismissive of the Congress, sit up and take notice.

Party and the Gandhis

The Congress will elect its next president in October. Who will it be, I cannot say. The rank and file, overwhelmingly, want that Mr Rahul Gandhi should take up the office from which he resigned in July 2019. That is their right. However, Mr Gandhi has made it clear that he has no desire to be the Congress president again.

The party leaders may make a valiant last effort to persuade Mr Gandhi to change his mind but, if he does not relent, they must respect the wishes of Mr Gandhi and move on. The electoral college must elect another person as president and draw the curtain on the interim presidency. In my view, the election of a non-Gandhi as Congress president will not mean that the party has abandoned the Gandhis or vice versa.

History Lessons

The history of the Congress party has valuable lessons. After the advent of Mahatma Gandhi on the Indian political scene, he was the acknowledged leader of the Congress party. He was the tallest among many tall leaders. During the period 1921–1948, fourteen different individuals occupied the office of Congress president and among them were giants such as C.R. Das, Sarojini Naidu, S. Srinivasa Iyengar, M.A. Ansari, Motilal Nehru, Jawaharlal Nehru, Vallabhbhai Patel, Rajendra Prasad, Subhas Chandra Bose, Abul Kalam Azad and Acharya Kripalani. The rank and file of the party, and even non-members, understood the subtle but important difference: that Mahatma Gandhi was the 'Leader of the Congress' and the other person was the 'President of the Congress'. One office/individual did not try to dominate the other.

A similar arrangement was in place in the years between 1948 and 1964: Jawaharlal Nehru was the acknowledged Leader of the Congress, while seven individuals occupied the chair of the President of the Congress. The period 1965 to 1984 was no different: Indira Gandhi was the Congress leader while eight individuals were Congress president.

In a large political party of a large country, the arrangement makes eminent sense. The leader's task is to provide leadership to the people, share a vision with them and inspire them to vote for the party. The president's main function is to fix the nuts and bolts of the organisation, keep it in good repair and make it a fighting-fit election machine. The two tasks are complementary. If a party finds one person to perform both tasks, that party is lucky; if it divides the duties between two individuals, that party is practical and wise.

Inspire, Rebuild

As I said, a leader must inspire. Mahatma Gandhi did so with his novel political thesis of non-violence, non-cooperation, civil disobedience and, ultimately, the Quit India movement. Jawaharlal Nehru fired the imagination of the people with the lofty ideas of non-alignment, secularism and socialism. Indira Gandhi urged the nation to dream big and took bold measures like bank nationalisation and housing for all. A.B. Vajpayee raised the sights of the nation with ambitious projects like the Golden Quadrilateral. An inspired turn of phrase ('tryst with destiny') or an electrifying slogan ('garibi hatao') or an expansive vision ('insaniyat, jamhuriat and Kashmiriyat') can raise the leader to lofty heights.

By contrast, a party president must be firmly grounded, guarding and nourishing the flock, and taking the hard decisions. The Congress party machinery is in serious disrepair and needs to be fixed urgently. This will require long hours on the road and longer hours with the party workers. The president must keep a close watch on the performance of every unit of the party from the booth to the block to the district to the state. The president must coddle and chastise the workers, reward and punish the leaders, and replace the obsolete or defective parts of the party machine. That is a 24×7 job, 364 days a year (the president's birthday excepted!). The key to a multiparty democracy and to a functional Parliament is the Congress. Absent the Congress, we may resign ourselves to a one-party State and an illusion of a democracy.

Whether the Congress will get a leader-cum-president or a leader and a president, will be known in the next six days. This will be a crucial week for the Congress party as well as for the country. On second thought, the unusual and obtrusive interest shown in the internal elections of the Congress party may not be entirely unjustified.

September 25, 2022

Neglect Duty, Start Controversy

I am proud of Ms Kasthuri. She introduced herself as belonging to a middle-class family and a good student who had studied in a school that followed the Tamil Nadu State Board syllabus. Then she dropped the bombshell that should have silenced Ms Nirmala Sitharaman, the finance minister. Responding to the FM's outburst, she said, 'I studied Hindi and later Sanskrit (not Tamil) as a subject, and I got every scholarship that was available to meritorious school students.' As I write this, Ms Sitharaman has not refuted Ms Kasthuri.

The wrangle was triggered by Ms Sitharaman's accusation – lips pursed, face angry, words harsh – that children who studied Hindi as a subject in schools in Tamil Nadu were denied merit scholarships and discriminated against. She let loose allegations: that when she was a young student in Tamil Nadu, anyone who studied Hindi was mocked at, abused in schools and on the streets, and virtually ostracised. She told the interviewer, Ms Marya Shakil, that 'nothing much has changed' in Tamil Nadu. She called the Tamil people 'civilised' but the hatred towards Hindi that stopped people from learning Hindi by choice was 'uncivilised'. She said she rejected the hatred towards Hindi whether it was because political parties owed their origin to the Justice Party or they believed in the 'Dravidian model'. Strong words, indeed. On the screen, she gave the impression that she was deliberately initiating a fight.

Parties Refute

The DMK and the AIADMK – the parties that ruled Tamil Nadu over the last fifty-five years – came down upon the FM like a tonne of bricks. The Congress spokesperson, Mr Mohan Kumaramangalam, challenged the FM to produce evidence of her charges. He rubbed it in by saying that the FM belonged to the No Data Available government.

But it was Ms Kasthuri who stole the show.

The *official* education policy of the government of Tamil Nadu is that it rejected the three-language formula and followed the two-language formula: Tamil and English in government schools. Both the DMK and the AIADMK have stuck to this policy. However, Hindi is offered as a language in thousands of aided and non-aided private schools and the government does not interfere with their decision. Besides, there are 1,417 schools affiliated to the CBSE, 76 affiliated to ICSE and 8 affiliated to IB. There are 41 Anglo-Indian schools. There are also 51 Kendriya Vidyalayas of the Central government. All of them offer Hindi as a subject.

The *unofficial* policy of state governments in the Hindi-speaking states is the one-language formula in government schools. The sole language is Hindi, both as the medium of instruction and as a subject of study. Among the second languages offered are Sanskrit, Punjabi, Marathi and Gujarati. English is supposed to be offered, but most schools do not have qualified English teachers and few students opt for English. There is not even a pretence of offering one of the South Indian languages. Private schools are happy to follow the example of government schools.

Effectively, therefore, it is a *one*-language policy in Hindi-speaking states; a *two*-language policy in states where the local language is not Hindi but a cognate language (for example Gujarati, Marathi, Punjabi); and the insistence on the *three*-language policy is only in respect of the southern Indian states.

Learning Hindi

Thousands of children in the South Indian states learn Hindi either by opting for it in schools that offer Hindi or through organisations like the Dakshin Bharat Hindi Prachar Sabha or Bharatiya Vidya Bhavan. Every year, thousands of students take the courses and the examinations conducted by the Hindi Prachar Sabha (established in 1918). In 2022, 2,50,000 candidates wrote the examinations at various levels in Tamil Nadu alone.

Moreover, migration has brought lakhs of Hindi-speaking people to the South Indian states. They are happy to speak Hindi in their homes, English at their workplaces and the local language (which they pick up) in public places.

Mischievous Plan

The FM's claim that there is hatred towards Hindi or that people who learn Hindi are mocked at or abused was never true and is not true now. The new front opened by the FM in Tamil Nadu appears to be part of a well-crafted strategy to manufacture an issue on which divisions can be easily exploited. The strategy is backed by huge funds. Desperate efforts are being made by the BJP to expand its footprint in Andhra Pradesh, Kerala and Tamil Nadu and to strengthen its presence in Karnataka and Telangana. Apparently, the FM has been tasked, or has volunteered, to stoke the fires, among them language. BJP cadres are already fighting street battles with Muslim groups. BJP's leaders in Kerala, Tamil Nadu, Telangana and Karnataka have been encouraged to be aggressive and provocative.

I am not surprised by the willingness of the FM to be on the front line. Having failed to win public esteem due to soaring unemployment, raging inflation, falling rupee, insensitive comments ('we don't eat onions') and frequent quarrels with the State governments on GST, prices of diesel and petrol, and sharing of tax revenues, she is perhaps trying to reinvent herself as a 'no-holds barred' politician who is willing to wade into controversies. I wish the FM good luck in her new avatar but I am pretty certain that, at every corner, she will encounter one among a growing tribe of confident and courageous Kasthuris.

October 2, 2022

Will Hindi and Hindu Own India?

On October 11, 2022 Mr Narendra Modi was in Ujjain to inaugurate the new 900-metre corridor at the Mahakal temple in Ujjain, Madhya Pradesh.

A Virtuoso Performance

Mr Modi is a devout Hindu. Most Indians are devout Hindus. Most others who are not Hindus are equally devout to another faith. When he went to the Mahakaleshwar temple, Mr Modi offered prayers and performed the rituals, and every minute of that was dutifully telecast live by all the channels that I surfed. At the sanctorum, he was draped in a golden angavastram and a saffron scarf. He had sandalwood paste on his forehead and a big tilak. When he addressed the gathering (I suppose nearly all Hindus), it was obvious that he had prepared well. He recalled the ancient cities and their great temples located all over the country. He quoted from Sanskrit scriptures. He spoke at length on the significance of Shiv bhakti. It was not clear if he had memorised his lines or he had a teleprompter before him (hidden from the TV camera). Whichever it be, it was a virtuoso performance.

It was not a routine inaugural speech. It was what is called a pravachan, a spiritual discourse by a Hindu preacher to an all-Hindu audience that loved every word. Mr Modi said that India was on a spiritual journey and 'we are restoring the spiritual glory of India'. He concluded his speech with the 'Jai Jai Mahakal' chant several times and the audience repeated the chant with great fervour. The message was clear. The India in Mr Modi's pages of history was a Hindu India and the India of Mr Modi's dreams will be a Hindu India.

Picture Imperfect

Everything seemed picture perfect. The only discordant reminder was that Mr Narendra Modi is not a private individual but the Hon'ble Prime Minister of India – a nation that is made up of Hindus (79.8 per cent), Muslims (14.2), Christians (2.3), Sikhs (1.7) and Others (2.0) – and he is obliged by the Constitution of India to act and speak for all the people of India. The India of the last 2,000 years was built, and the India of our dreams will be built, by every Indian regardless of his/her faith. That is why the Constitution stressed 'equality' and the Constitution was amended to explicitly stress 'secularism' that was always implicit in a Republican document.

I am happy that the prime minister was at the inaugural in Ujjain, but I would like to see the prime minister at the renovation/consecration of a Mosque or a Church. I am happy that the prime minister spoke eloquently about the spiritual journey of the Hindus, but I would like the prime minister to celebrate the spiritual journey of Muslims, Christians and others too. I am happy that the prime minister quoted from Hindu scriptures, but I would like the prime minister to quote, on occasion, a stirring passage from the Bible or a solemn verse from the Koran or a soulful hymn from the Guru Granth Sahib.

Provoking a Conflict

While the prime minister was celebrating the Hindu faith, the home minister was quietly pushing the Hindi language. The home minister is the ex-officio Chair of the Committee on Official Language. Its 11th Report was presented to the President on September 9, 2022 and kept under wraps – until The Print broke the story about its contents. The contents will certainly cause reverberations in the non-Hindi speaking states of India.

Look at the main recommendations as reported by The Print:

- Hindi will be the compulsory medium of instruction in Kendriya Vidyalayas, IITs, IIMs and central universities. Question: will Hindi be the medium of instruction in Kendriya Vidyalayas, IITs, IIMs and central universities located in non-Hindi-speaking states as well? Will Hindi be the sole medium of instruction or an alternative medium of instruction?
- Hindi will replace English as the language of examinations for government recruitment. Question: will those who do not know Hindi be barred from writing the examinations for government recruitment?
- Explanations will be sought from government officers who deliberately don't work in Hindi. Question: will an officer whose language is Bengali or Odiya or Tamil be compelled to learn Hindi and do his official work in Hindi?
- English as a medium of instruction will be retained only where it is absolutely necessary and will be gradually replaced by Hindi. Question: will the parent and the student no longer have the right to choose the language in which the student will study and be taught?
- Knowledge of Hindi will be ensured for selection of employees in the government. Question: will a non-Hindi-speaking person be refused a government job on the ground that he/she does not know Hindi?

- 50 per cent of the government's advertisement budget should be allocated to Hindi advertisements. Question: if the remaining 50 per cent is allocated to advertisements in all other languages (including English), will it not hasten the withering away of the non-Hindi media?
- The propagation of Hindi should be made a constitutional obligation of all state governments. Question: will a state government that refused to propagate Hindi be dismissed?

If I were an Assamese or a Malayali, I would feel that I am a half-citizen. If I were also a Muslim or Christian, I would feel that I am a non-citizen.

October 16, 2022

Hijab: Point and Counterpoint

The hijab: To wear, or not to wear, that is the question.

The question was answered by two Honourable Judges of the Supreme Court but, at the end of the day on October 13, there were two Opinions, but no Answer. As a result, Ms Aishat Shifa and Ms Tehrina Begum, born and raised in a small town called Kundapura, district Udupi, Karnataka, are unable to resume their studies in Government Pre-University College, Kundapura. Both students were in the second year. Since the day they had joined the college in the previous year, they had worn the hijab – a scarf that covered the head and neck but left the face visible. The hijab was worn in addition to the prescribed uniform. On February 3, 2022, they were stopped at the gate and told that they would have to remove the hijab before entering the college. They refused, they were denied entry, and that is where the matter stands eight months later.

Hijab Is No Different

A woman wearing the hijab causes no offence to anybody. It is not against public order, decency, morality or health. Irrespective of the religious significance, a woman wearing the hijab is not very different from women in India who cover their head with the pallu of their sari or a dupatta. Men wear turbans. Sikh men cover their heads with a pagri. Many states of India have distinctive headgear worn on special occasions (for example the Mysuru peta).

What is the central issue of the controversy? Amidst the screaming headlines, the cacophony on television, the flood of comments, trolls and memes in the social media and the lofty pronouncements of worthy leaders, the central issue has been lost. In my view, the issue boils down to one word: CHOICE.

Fascinating Fencing

There are two approaches to the question of 'choice' concerning wearing of the hijab. I may illustrate the two approaches by quoting from the opinions of the two Honourable Judges, Justice Hemant Gupta and Justice Sudhanshu Dhulia:

- Justice Gupta: 'The practice of wearing of hijab may be a "religious practice" or an "essential religious practice" or it may be social conduct for the women of Islamic faith ... The religious belief cannot be carried to a secular school maintained out of state funds.'
- Justice Dhulia: 'Whether wearing hijab is an essential religious practice or not is not essential for the determination of this dispute. If the belief is sincere, and it harms no one else, there can be no justifiable reasons for banning hijab in a classroom.'
- Justice Gupta: '... the decision of the state government mandating the College Development Committee to ensure the students wear the uniform as prescribed does not violate the freedom guaranteed under Article 19(1)(a), rather reinforces the right to equality under Article 14.'
- Justice Dhulia: 'Asking a pre-university schoolgirl to take off her hijab at her school gate is an invasion of her privacy and dignity. It is clearly violative of the

Fundamental Right given to her under Articles 19(1)(a) and 21 of the Constitution.'

- Justice Gupta: 'Therefore, the Preambular goal of justice, liberty, equality or fraternity would be better served by removing any religious differences, inequalities, and treating students alike before they attain the age of adulthood.'
- Justice Dhulia: 'This is the time to foster in them sensitivity, empathy and understanding towards different religions, languages and cultures. This is the time when they should learn not to be alarmed by our diversity but to rejoice and celebrate this diversity.'
- Justice Gupta: 'If they choose not to attend classes due to the uniform that has been prescribed, it is a voluntary act of such students and cannot be said to be in violation of Article 29 by the state.'
- Justice Dhulia: 'If she wants to wear hijab even inside her classroom, she cannot be stopped, if it is worn as a matter of her choice, as it may be the only way her conservative family will permit her to go to school, and in those cases, her hijab is her ticket to education.'

Choice or Rule

Some commentators have complained that when there is a movement for shedding the hijab in conservative Iran, it is surprising that a section of the Muslim community should defend the right of girls to wear the hijab in classrooms in modern India. The criticism is completely misplaced. On a closer look, the controversy is the same in both Iran and India: it is about 'choice'. It is like the controversy in America over the woman's choice of abortion.

The controversy is between 'Choice' and 'Rule'. 'Choice' represents freedom, dignity, privacy and diversity.

'Rule' is often a product of majoritarianism, intolerance and drive for uniformity.

'Choice' will yield to 'Rule' in certain situations that attract the grounds contained in Article 19(2) or Article 25(1) of the Constitution – public order, decency, morality and health – and in certain other provisions of Part III of the Constitution (Fundamental Rights). Absent such grounds, 'Choice' must prevail.

Justice Sudhanshu Dhulia upheld 'Choice' because the hijab may be the girls' only ticket to education. Justice Hemant Gupta upheld the 'Rule', although the state showed no compelling necessity.

Let the larger Bench of the Supreme Court lay down the law. Meanwhile, each one of you must decide whether you stand with 'Choice' or 'Rule'.

October 23, 2022

Gujarat: A Model Not to Follow

Prime Minister Narendra Modi has visited Gujarat several times since October and he is expected to pay more visits in November before the state goes to elections on December 1 and 5. He has held programmes in practically every one of the 33 districts of Gujarat. As long as the Election Commission was indulgent, the PM was on an 'inaugural' spree. These were billed as 'official' events, but there was nothing 'official' about the contents of the PM's speeches. In all his speeches (in Gujarat, elsewhere in India and even abroad) there is one recurring theme: the history of modern, resurgent India began in 2014. By the same reasoning, the history of modern, resurgent Gujarat began in 2001. If there is something jarring in those statements (Gujarat, even before India?), I leave it to you to crack the puzzle.

According to the PM, Gujarat is the model for India. He is one step away from claiming that India is the model for the world. The people of Gujarat will vote on the PM's claim in early December. Unfortunately, the people of the world will not have an opportunity to vote on the other claim. I suppose it is their misfortune.

Not to Be Envied

Let's examine the Gujarat model. I noticed some unique features:

- The BJP government has been in power but, since 2016, there have been three chief ministers. Among the three, the longest serving was Mr Vijay Rupani

– from 2016 to 2021 – but he left such an indelible mark that he was unceremoniously removed from office along with his entire council of ministers. 'Revolving door chief ministers' is the preferred model for modern, resurgent Gujarat (precedents: Karnataka, Uttarakhand).

- Another feature of the Gujarat model is the 'double engine' government. You may think the double engines are 'PM & CM'. You are wrong. The double engines are 'PM & HM'. Nothing moves in Gujarat unless the double engines are fired. When the rest of India follows the Gujarat model, we can get rid of state governments, and get rid of the states as well, and create 'One India, One Government'.

Pride in Decline

- A notable feature of the Gujarat model is declining growth rates, but ascending Gujarati pride. The state GDP's growth rates in four years have been the following:

  2017–18: 10.7 per cent, 2018–19: 8.9, 2019–20: 7.3 and 2020–21: –1.9. You may ask if the all-India GDP's growth rates were on the decline since 2017–18. The answer is 'of course, yes'. It is because India emulated the Gujarat model. If post-pandemic, there was a bounce in Gujarat's GSDP of 2021–22, there was a bounce in the all-India GDP too. What Gujarat did yesterday, India will do tomorrow.

- Another feature that India will adopt is the principle of 'No apology, no resignation'. The Morbi bridge's collapse killed 135 people including 53 children. The scale of the tragedy did not call for the PM to address the media and take questions. The High Court pointed out that there was a one and one-quarter page agreement; no Expression of Interest; no tender; no pre-qualifications; no competitive bids; no conditions; no fitness certificate after the bridge got a fresh coat of paint (so-called repair); and yet the bridge was opened to the public. As a principle, Gujarat believes in 'no apologies and no resignations'. In the future, India too will follow this principled principle of no accountability.

- Like a pride of lions (preferably from the Gir forest), there is pride in numbers. The numbers enhance Gujarati asmita (pride). For example, look at this table of promised investment and actual investment in Gujarat:

Year	Promised investment (Rs crore)	Actual investment (Rs crore)
2003	66,068	30,746
2005	1,06,160	37,939
2007	4,65,309	1,07,897
2009	12,39,562	1,04,590
2011	20,83,047	29,813

India's asmita too will be enhanced as the gap widens between promise and reality.

Women, Youth and Children

- Gujarat is a model of how (not) to treat women, starting with the girl child. The sex ratio (female to male) is 919 as against the all-India average of 943. While the labour participation rate is 41.0 per cent, the LPF for females is 23.4 per cent. Where are the missing girl children? And if they survive, 76 per cent do not work outside their homes.

- The Gujarat model does not burden youth with work. The unemployment rate among youth aged 20–24 years is 12.49 per cent. They are well rested before the elections.
- Gujarat is a model of (not) caring for children, their nutrition and their health. Among children, 39 per cent are stunted and 39.7 per cent are underweight. Wasted children amount to 25.1 per cent. In these indicators, Gujarat ranks between 26 and 29 among the 30 states of India.
- The Gujarat model faithfully followed the RSS's dictum that 'all Indians living in this country are Hindus'. Consequently, Muslims constituting 9.67 per cent of the state's population are Hindus. Therefore, under the Gujarat model, the BJP has not fielded a Muslim candidate (in 182 seats) in the quinquennial Assembly elections since 1995.

The Gujarat model must be exported to other states and other countries as well. A vote for the Gujarat model will ensure that goal is achieved. Amen.

November 20, 2022

Wannabe Chief Ministers

There are 28 States in India. Puducherry and Delhi are two Union Territories with a legislature. Jammu and Kashmir was a State until it was dismembered into two Union Territories. Every state has a Governor at its head.

Elections are held to the State Legislative Assembly. The members elected from territorial constituencies belong to different parties. The leader of the largest party is invited to form the government and he/she is sworn in as the chief minister. The CM is the elected leader of the people of the state. On the CM's advice, the ministers are appointed. That is the Westminster parliamentary system. India followed the system since Independence and aberrations were quickly corrected.

One Government

But there are people who do not like the Westminster system. By extension, they don't like states; they don't like elected legislatures; and they don't like chief ministers. In sum, they would like to get rid of state governments. If China with 1,426 million people can have *one government*, why not India with 1,412 million people? The tribe against the Westminster model is growing. Some of the tribe have been appointed Governors of states.

A Governor of a state is a titular head (like the British monarch) and the government is run in the name of the Governor. The Constitution prescribes – and limits – the powers of the Governor (Article 163):

> There shall be a Council of Ministers with the Chief Minister as the head to aid and advise the Governor in the exercise of his functions except in so far as he is by or under the Constitution required to exercise his functions or any of them in his discretion.

The language is plain and simple. Considered in the background of the Westminster model that we adopted, the meaning of Article 163 admits of no doubt. Like the monarch in England, the Governor has no real powers. He may act in his discretion only in matters where the Constitution required him to do so. Still, there were doubting Thomases. Justice Krishna Iyer set them right in his judgement in *Samsher Singh vs State of Punjab*:

> We declare the law of this branch of our Constitution to be that the President and Governor … shall … exercise their formal constitutional powers only upon and in accordance with the advice of their Ministers save in a few well-known exceptional situations.

Crossing the Limits

Yet we have Governors who wish to lord over chief ministers. They are wannabe chief ministers.

- The Governor's assent is required for a Bill to become law. Article 200 provides that the Governor may assent or withhold assent or reserve it for the consideration of the President. If assent to a Bill is withheld, the Bill must be returned to the Legislature for reconsideration. If the Bill is passed again, with or without amendments, the Governor is obliged to give his assent. There are Governors who simply 'sit' on the Bills. The specious reason is that the Governor is 'considering' the Bill. How many times will a Governor read a Bill and consider it? If he is incapable of understanding Bills, he should resign citing his incapacity.

- Governors contradict state governments. There is a state government that is opposed to the New Education Policy (NEP) and the so-called three-language formula. The Governor of the state contradicted the state government and extolled the virtues of the NEP and the three-language formula. The Governor also contradicted the state government on other issues. The MPs of that state, supported by the state government, submitted a signed memorandum to the President to recall the Governor.
- Governors make extraneous and provocative remarks. A Governor said that Chhatrapati Shivaji was an 'icon of the olden days'. The whole state was up in arms and the chief minister's party, otherwise friendly to the Governor and the Central government, demanded his recall.
- Governors make unsavoury remarks. A Governor said of the chief minister that 'If the CM was not aware that someone from his office was directing the Vice Chancellor to appoint a relative, it shows how incompetent he is. If he knew about it, then he is equally guilty.' Earlier, the same Governor had said he knew about the chief minister's past political record and, on one occasion, the young party leader (now CM) had to change his clothes (implying that he had wet himself).
- Governors have been rewarded for 'welcoming' leaders belonging to the party opposed to the chief minister and have been called 'abhibhavak' or guardian. On the other hand, Governors have been shown the door for observing constitutional norms.

The Itch

Why do Governors behave like wannabe chief ministers? Dr C. Rangarajan, a distinguished economist and former Governor of RBI, who was also Governor of a state, has this to say in his book *Forks in the Road*:

> Purely political appointees have a problem in dealing with chief ministers who do not belong to their party. There is a tendency to administer pinpricks… Quite clearly, two centres of power in the state were not contemplated in the Constitution. Furthermore, individuals who are appointed as governor have often held responsible positions in the past. They were 'hands-on' administrators and were used to exercising power. The 'itch' to act is evident sometimes. This is what they must learn to control.

Not likely, because the anti-Westminster tribe loves wannabe chief ministers as Governors.

November 27, 2022

Rays of Sunshine

In many elections in the past, incumbency was considered a millstone around a party's neck. After the dominant Congress era ended in 1967, several governments in the states were defeated and, led by regional parties, non-Congress parties came to power. The era of non-Congress governments at the Centre began in 1977.

The saga of alternating governments started in Kerala. Since the 1990s, we have seen alternating governments in Rajasthan, Himachal Pradesh, Uttar Pradesh, Madhya Pradesh, Bihar, Andhra Pradesh, Karnataka and Tamil Nadu.

Defying Incumbency

However, there have been examples of tall leaders defying incumbency. M.G. Ramachandran and his party, the AIADMK, won three elections in a row from 1977 in Tamil Nadu until his death in 1987. J. Jayalalithaa and her party, the AIADMK, won two successive elections in Tamil Nadu in 2011 and 2016. Mr Naveen Patnaik and his party, the BJD, have won five successive elections since 2,000. The most spectacular – and daunting – example has been the BJP that has won six successive elections in Gujarat since 1998 (and since 2002 under the leadership of Mr Narendra Modi as chief minister or as the de facto leader).

It appears that in certain situations and under certain leaders, incumbency has turned out to be a strength than a weakness. This phenomenon requires careful analysis by political observers, social psychologists and psephologists.

My prima facie observations are the following:

1. Parties which are in government amass a huge election war-chest during the five years in government, a thing unheard of when tall leaders like K. Kamaraj, S. Nijalingappa, K. Brahmananda Reddy, E.M.S. Namboodiripad, Hitendra Desai, Y.B. Chavan, M.L. Sukhadia or Jyoti Basu (among others) were in power.
2. Ruling parties do not hesitate to politicise the bureaucracy, especially the police forces. Nowhere is it more visible than in Gujarat and Uttar Pradesh. In the recent by-election in Rampur Assembly constituency, the polling percentage was approx. 32 per cent while in Khatauli Assembly constituency of the same state the percentage was approx. 56 per cent. In the Mainpuri Lok Sabha constituency, the percentage was approx. 53 per cent. The Samajwadi Party has alleged that the low voting in Rampur was mainly attributable to the role of the police.

Adding Technology, Muscle

3. Clever and far-sighted political parties have used technology extensively to strengthen and fine-tune their organisation. The BJP, and a few other parties, have been able to constitute booth committees to micro-manage the elections, especially on polling day. The BJP has been able to take micro-management to the level of management of the voters on each page of the electoral roll.
4. Ruling parties that have a well-structured party organisation add 'muscle' to the organisation. In the run-up to the elections, defectors from other parties, including serving legislators and notorious

musclemen, are enticed to cross over to the ruling party. Money is an undoubted enticement. More than money, it is the 'amnesty' offered in respect of ongoing investigations into crimes that does the trick. Suddenly, all investigations by the agencies stop in the case of a defector to the ruling party.

5. In the past few years, the ruling party has used religion as a polarising factor. This is done in many ways, some brazen and some subtle. For example, the BJP did not nominate any candidate from the Muslim community in the elections in Gujarat (2012, 2017 and 2022) and in Uttar Pradesh (2022), although Muslims constitute 9.7 per cent of the population of Gujarat and 20 per cent of Uttar Pradesh. The refusal to nominate a Muslim candidate sends a signal to the other communities and inevitably polarises the electorate.
6. The failure of governance of the ruling party is sought to be drowned by a high-decibel campaign that is magnified manyfold by a frightened – and also fawning – media. An independent media is a thing of the past. Practically, all media outlets (TV and newspapers) are owned and controlled by corporates. The social media is relatively free but is swamped by fake news, fake videos, trolls and bots.

Winners Can Lose

Besides the above, I am sure there are other factors at the level of the larger society that are unique to the history and culture of each state. In my view, a strange peace and silence has descended on Gujarat and Uttar Pradesh. Is it, as John Kennedy observed presciently, 'the peace of the grave and the silence of the slave'? I sincerely hope it is not so. Dissent is suppressed by the State and practically blanked out by the media. If these trends lead to an eerie silence and peace, it will mean that we are hastening the day when India will be an electoral democracy but not a Constitutional democracy.

The recently concluded elections hold lessons for both winners and losers. The common lesson is that the winner had a strong party organisation, dedicated cadres, a spirited campaign and micro-management. In Gujarat, the BJP alone had all four factors going in its favour and defied incumbency. On the contrary, the principal challenger in Himachal Pradesh (Congress) and Delhi Corporation (AAP) had all four factors going in its favour and incumbency proved fatal.

Irrespective of the political party that won or lost, the victory of three parties in three elections are like the rays of sunshine amidst growing darkness.

December 11, 2022

Man, Mission and Message

I know that people find it hard to believe that a political leader can embark upon a yatra (march) without a political objective. History has many examples of marches: Adi Shankara (700 CE, disputed, religious), Mao Zedong (1934–35, military), Mahatma Gandhi (1930, civil disobedience) and Martin Luther King (1963, 1965, civil rights).

On January 29, 2023, Mr Rahul Gandhi's Bharat Jodo Yatra covered about 4,000 kilometres in 135 days. Whatever one's political persuasion, or even if one is not political, one cannot dispute that the yatra was an unparalleled demonstration of grit, determination and physical endurance.

Why BJP's Alarm?

Mr Gandhi has repeatedly said that his yatra had no political or electoral objective and the sole objective was to spread the message of love, fraternity, communal harmony and unity. These cannot be neatly labelled as 'political' or 'electoral'; hence, the BJP and other critics are flummoxed. The BJP has found irrational grounds to criticise the yatra. Its minister of health struck upon the puerile idea of 'the danger of spread of coronavirus' to make Mr Gandhi abort the yatra.

Mr Gandhi was not deterred. He carried on regardless of the criticism. He reached out to the people, especially the youth, women, children, farmers, labourers and the people on the margins of society. He found confirmation of his beliefs that there is widespread poverty and unemployment in India; that every section of the people is groaning under the weight of inflation; that there are messengers of hate in society; and that Indian society is more divided than ever before. In street meetings and large rallies, he expressed his anguish at the deep divisions.

Why is the BJP alarmed by the overwhelming response that Mr Gandhi received during the yatra? Some things have to be seen to be believed. I walked with Mr Gandhi in Kanyakumari, Mysuru and Delhi. There were l-a-r-g-e crowds at every place. So it was in every State and at every place: I have seen photographs and videos. No one was bused to any point on the route. No one was paid to participate. No one was promised food packets. There were thousands of youth who walked. There were hundreds of middle-aged and old persons and children, on either side of the road, waving, throwing flowers and cheering. Nearly everyone had a mobile phone and took pictures.

There were special people like artistes, writers, scholars, political persons, disabled, etc. As far as I was concerned, the ordinary folk were the most important part of the yatra. They were sending a silent message that they had heard and understood the message of Mr Gandhi: that India was too divided and surcharged with hate and violence and the answer to the collapse of the social compact was embracing love, fraternity, communal harmony and unity.

Presence of Poor

What hit me hard was the number of poor people everywhere. The deniers – if they were present – would have realised how many thousands were poor and that the cause of poverty was unemployment. According to the Global Multidimensional Poverty Index 2022, the proportion of poor in India is 16 per cent of the population, that is, 22.4 crore people. That does not mean that the rest are rich. The bar of poverty is low at Rs 1,286 per month (urban areas) and Rs 1,089 per month (rural areas). The unemployment rate was 8.3 per cent in December 2022.

I am certain there were hundreds in the crowds who had voted for the BJP or a non-Congress party in the last elections, but I did not see any hostility on their faces.

Many were curious, but almost everyone had a glimmer of hope in the eyes: will this yatra lead to a better tomorrow?

Why BJP's Hostility?

Why is the BJP hostile to the idea of spreading love and communal harmony? Because, despite sabka saath sabka vikas, the BJP has systematically excluded the Muslims and Christians and has disdain for the other minorities. There is no Muslim in the Union council of ministers. Of the 303 MPs of the Lok Sabha and the 92 MPs of the Rajya Sabha belonging to the BJP, there is no member who is Muslim. The sole Muslim judge in the Supreme Court retired on January 5, 2023. BJP supporters find excuses to provoke violence such as wearing a hijab, inter-faith marriage, so-called love jihad, transporting cows, serving non-vegetarian food in hostels, etc. Lynching happens. Christian churches are vandalised. Ask any police officer in an area where there is a mix of the majority and minority communities and he or she will tell you that he/she is policing a tinderbox.

What about the man – Mr Gandhi – himself? The experience of the yatra may have influenced Mr Gandhi, but I know that it has brought about a remarkable change in the way people perceive him. Even BJP members reluctantly admit his grit, determination and willingness to bear physical stress. Dozens of people (who I know did not vote for the Congress) have told me that they see Mr Gandhi in a new light. It is obvious to me that the man's message has percolated to all sections of the people.

The Man has earned respect. The Mission was an undoubted success. The Message has spread far and wide. That is good, for now.

January 29, 2023

Opposition Unity Platform: Stoop to Conquer

The oldest party in the country is the Indian National Congress. The biggest party in the country is the Bharatiya Janata Party, also by far the richest. In the last Lok Sabha elections (2019), all BJP candidates together won 37.4 per cent of the votes that were polled. The Congress candidates won 19.5 per cent of the votes. There are regional and state-specific parties that are quite influential and rule many states.

India's electoral map is a multicoloured political mosaic. The BJP's aim – not concealed – is to make it a monochromatic mosaic. The Opposition parties' (those who are opposed to the BJP) goal is to replace the BJP at the Centre and form a liberal, progressive and inclusive government.

The Challenge

In every election since 2014, the BJP seeks votes not in the name of the party or its manifesto but in the name of Mr Narendra Modi. It has gone to the extent of appealing to the voters of Karnataka – the state will elect a new government on May 10 – to 'hand over Karnataka to Modi'. For the BJP, it is Mr Modi who is the candidate in every constituency. The BJP thinks that 'Modi everywhere' is enough to achieve its aim.

As of today, it appears that the Opposition parties do not have a common leader/candidate behind whom they are willing to rally. This may change, but we are looking at the position today. Minus this seeming disadvantage, the Opposition parties have many pluses and strengths, and this essay is intended to explore how the Opposition parties can leverage their strengths.

Some extreme options are ruled out. The Opposition parties will not, and cannot, unite to form a single new party, a la 1977, when the Janata Party was formed. None of the Opposition parties will cede the entire space in a state to another party. Despite appeals to forbear, AAP contested the elections in Uttarakhand (2022) and Karnataka (2023) and TMC in Goa (2022). So while total Opposition unity is desirable, it does not seem feasible.

Congress party is the lead		**Another party is the lead**		**BJP-friendly party is the lead**		**Unclear who is the lead**	
Madhya Pradesh	29	Uttar Pradesh	80	Andhra Pradesh	25	Maharashtra	48
Karnataka	28	West Bengal	42	Odisha	21	Tripura	2
Gujarat	26	Bihar	40	Manipur	2	Jammu and Kashmir	6
Rajasthan	25	Tamil Nadu	39	Meghalaya	2		
Kerala*	20	Telangana	17	Mizoram	1		
Assam	14	Delhi	7	Nagaland	1		
Jharkhand*	14			Sikkim	1		
Chhattisgarh	11						
Puducherry*	1						
Lakshadweep*	1						
Daman and Diu	1						
Dadra and Nagar Haveli	1						
Chandigarh	1						
Andaman and Nicobar	1						

Congress party is the lead		Another party is the lead	BJP-friendly party is the lead	Unclear who is the lead
Goa	2			
Arunachal Pradesh	2			
Himachal Pradesh	4			
Uttarakhand	5			
Haryana	10			
Punjab	13			
Total	**209**	**225**	**53**	**56**

* In these states or union territories, there are also other political parties which are opposed to the BJP, namely, CPI-M, JMM, NCP and DMK

Opposition Unity Platform

The alternative is an Opposition Unity Platform (OUP). An OUP will need each party to make concessions to others and gain from the concessions made by the others. The outline of the scheme is roughly as follows: create four columns of states and union territories and put each state/UT in the appropriate column (the number denotes the number of Lok Sabha seats).

Of course, it must be acknowledged that the BJP is more dominant than the 'Lead' Opposition party in many of the states (it has 302 MPs in the Lok Sabha).

In my view, if an OUP is formed, the Congress can legitimately expect to take the lead in fighting the BJP in about 209 seats. Likewise, another Opposition party among SP, TMC, RJD, JD(U), DMK, BRS and AAP can take the lead in about 225 seats. In three states, there are two or three parties that are in a position to take the lead to challenge the BJP. In seven states with 53 seats, the winner may turn out to be a covert ally of the BJP.

Cardinal Rule

Next step: all parties on the OUP must willingly subscribe to the rule that while the Lead party will contest the majority of the seats in the state concerned, the Lead party will be obliged to give the seat to the candidate who has the best chance of winning the seat irrespective of the Opposition party to which the candidate may belong. Sometimes, this may mean denying the seat to the Lead party's own member. The goal is not to maximise the number of seats that each Lead party may win but to defeat the BJP's candidates in the maximum number of seats. All Opposition parties must stoop to conquer.

The arithmetic is simple. The BJP is in a position to win over 150 seats. Among the Opposition parties, the Congress alone is in a position to win over 100 seats. Every other Opposition party, even if there is a wave in its favour, can win a maximum of 40 seats but, together, they can win up to 150 seats. The BJP is not unbeatable. If the Opposition parties willingly subscribe to the plan that I have outlined, there is a credible path to victory.

April 30, 2023

About the Author

P. Chidambaram has been a member of India's Parliament for many terms since he was first elected in 1984. He was a minister in the governments of Rajiv Gandhi, P.V. Narasimha Rao, H.D. Deve Gowda, I.K. Gujral and Manmohan Singh. In the UPA government, he held the portfolios of finance (2004–2008 and 2012–2014) and home (2008–2012).

Since 2016, P. Chidambaram has been a member of the Council of States (Rajya Sabha) representing the Congress party.

He is also a Senior Advocate practising in the Supreme Court of India and various High Courts.

He is a well-known columnist. When in the Opposition benches, he has regularly written a weekly column titled 'Across the Aisle'. It is published every week in the *Indian Express* and the *Financial Express*. Currently, the column is also published every week in ten Indian newspapers in ten languages. Several collections of the columns have been published over the years.

P. Chidambaram hails from Tamil Nadu and was elected as a member of Parliament from Sivagangai constituency of that state.

His wife, Nalini, is also a Senior Advocate. His son, Karti Chidambaram, currently represents Sivagangai constituency in the Lok Sabha. The other members of his family are Karti's wife, Dr Srinidhi Chidambaram, a medical doctor, and a granddaughter, Aditi.

P. Chidambaram is a member of the Congress Working Committee, the highest decision-making body of the Congress party.

